REFLECTIVE PRACTICE FO
PROFESSIONAL DEVELOPI

Reflective Practice for Professional Development provides an accessible introduction to the theory and practice of reflection. In ten concise chapters it explores how reflecting on experiences can be used for professional development and help progress knowledge and skills.

Using scenarios, questions and stories, the reader is encouraged to apply the content to their own context, demonstrating the importance of reflection in helping us to make sense as well as make the most of our professional experience. Exploring key themes such as the importance of criticality, models of reflection and connections between thought, language and actions, it considers the ways in which reflection can widen perspectives, generate deeper understanding of professional challenges and enhance creativity.

Full of practical tools and approaches for enriching and recording reflections, this insightful book aims to simplify reflective practice for teachers. It is an ideal guide for anyone who needs to build reflection into their practice or their studies.

Carol Thompson is Senior Lecturer and Advanced Researcher in the School of Teacher Education at the University of Bedfordshire. She has over 20 years' experience of working with Trainee Teachers and Mentors and is author of several books in this field, including *The Magic of Mentoring* and the *Trainee Teacher's Handbook*.

REFLECTIVE PRACTICE FOR PROFESSIONAL DEVELOPMENT

A Guide for Teachers

Carol Thompson

Routledge
Taylor & Francis Group

LONDON AND NEW YORK

First published 2022
by Routledge
2 Park Square, Milton Park, Abingdon, Oxon OX14 4RN

and by Routledge
605 Third Avenue, New York, NY 10158

Routledge is an imprint of the Taylor & Francis Group, an informa business

British Library Cataloguing-in-Publication Data
A catalogue record for this book is available from the British Library

Library of Congress Cataloging-in-Publication Data
Names: Thompson, Carol, author.
Title: Reflective practice for professional development : a guide for teachers / Carol
    Thompson.
Description: Abingdon, Oxon ; New York : Routledge, 2022. | Includes bibliographical
    references and index.
Identifiers: LCCN 2021013972 | ISBN 9780367521783 (hardback) | ISBN
    9780367521813 (paperback) | ISBN 9781003056812 (ebook)
Subjects: LCSH: Reflective learning. | Reflective teaching. | Teachers–Training of. |
    Career development.
Classification: LCC LB1027.23 .T546 2022 | DDC 371.14/4–dc23
LC record available at https://lccn.loc.gov/2021013972

ISBN: 978-0-367-52178-3 (hbk)
ISBN: 978-0-367-52181-3 (pbk)
ISBN: 978-1-003-05681-2 (ebk)

DOI: 10.4324/9781003056812

Typeset in Interstate
by Apex Covantage, LLC

For my most loyal boy, Oscar.

CONTENTS

FIGURES

TABLES

ACKNOWLEDGEMENT

Thanks to my good friend Russell Collins, who thoughtfully kept copies of all of my work and patiently read my chapters in order to offer alternative perspectives. Both of these things offered a great sense of security that I am very grateful for.

INTRODUCTION

Most of us inhabit the world of routines, daily activities filling pockets of time in surprisingly similar ways. In our professional lives we have a multitude of tasks to complete and regular scheduled events that form part of these daily, weekly and monthly commitments. These events are woven into the fabric of our work so firmly we rarely question them. Similarly, systems and processes within the workplace provide the architecture for occupation; they create activities to complete, deadlines to meet and sometimes a set of attitudes and values to adopt. In addition to these things we form our own routines in professional practice, perhaps following a particular order for managing a meeting or teaching a class; so much so, these routines become embedded as a set of rules. We do things this way or that and very often forget the reasons why.

We could argue that routines have been created for good reason. When we undertake a new activity for the first time, we tend to think through our approach to it and if we are lucky, that approach works. So what happens then? Chances are, if it works it becomes part of our habitus and we do the same as yesterday, tomorrow and next month. This will probably serve us well, for a while at least, but what happens when things move on, when contexts change or when a world-changing event impacts on our day-to-day lives in ways we never imagined?

Although most people undertaking professional roles are very familiar with the process of evaluating practice, this usually takes place as part of the formal systems' machinery and as a result has a very definite purpose. This is reflection driven by a distinct end goal, perhaps the need to create evaluation documentation or to evidence competence. It looks at practice but must do so following a generic format and focussing on specific aspects, the importance of which is usually determined by other people. It is an evaluation of course, but an evaluation limited by protocol and process.

How many of us regularly take the time to truly reflect? To do more than simply gather our thoughts or briefly evaluate an event but to delve into meanings or to chase assumptions? It is this type of reflection, guided by the individual, that leads to perspective change and the potential for transformation, as it is done for no other reason than to explore, challenge and learn.

In the book *Vanity Fair*, Thackeray explored the events of day-to-day life and illustrated human frailties through his characters, suggesting that: 'The world is a looking glass and gives back to every man the reflection of his own face' (Thackeray, 1847: 17). His book was intended as a mirror so that readers may see something of themselves in its pages, and the

DOI: 10.4324/9781003056812-1

use of humour allowed them to do so in a way that was accepting of what might be seen as weaknesses. Reflection, whilst based on the desire to see ourselves as we are, should be accompanied by acceptance, kindness and perhaps humour, and this is an idea that has guided the content of the following chapters.

When we look in the mirror what we see represents a moment in time clouded by current focus, expectations or the way we 'filter' information. The same is true when we think about our professional practice; very often we see what we expect to see, and as a result we don't always question it. Reflective practice provides insight into actions and some clarity around initial thoughts and behaviours. It offers a platform from which to objectively explore our experiences and in doing so informs future action. It is a key professional skill, yet it is one that is often not executed effectively. This may be because managing reflection is something which is not as familiar as it could be.

Reflection itself calls for consideration of the abstract as well as the tangible; the process is personal and the outcomes unique. Any reflection is subject to interpretation and any interpretation is influenced by a myriad of contextual factors – so there is no 'one size fits all', we need to employ a range of skills to get the most from the process. In the following chapters we will explore the reasons why reflection is important to the development of professional knowledge and skills and will discuss a range of practical strategies that can be used to enhance reflective practice. Although the words cannot be compared to the eloquence of Thackeray, in a way this book has a similar aim to that of *Vanity Fair*, in that the content is framed by the events of day-to-day life. In doing this, it is hoped that this also offers something of a mirror so that readers may be able to link the ideas presented to real life and that they are able to do so in a way that is objective, has the potential to inform and, where necessary, change what they do.

Reference

Thackeray, W. M. (1847) *Vanity Fair: A Novel without a Hero*. London: Bradbury & Evans.

Figure 1.1 Chapter mindmap

1 Why should we reflect?

According to Heraclitus change is a constant in life. The suggestion that 'It is not possible to step into the same river twice' (Khan, 1979: 169) illustrates the idea that water is constantly flowing, new water arriving as the old departs, making the conditions of the river dynamic. Heraclitus probably had a point – just look at the advances in technology over the last 20 years for examples of how quickly things can change. In the year 2000, Tony Blair was Prime Minister, J. K. Rowling published Harry Potter and in the early noughties, the iPod was invented, Facebook was launched and YouTube was created. Change is all around us, impacting on our personal and professional lives and yet there is often a reluctance to reflect on yesterday in order to effect positive change for tomorrow. Our fast-paced society has driven most of us into a state of constant action and our days are filled to the brim – so much so that we rarely stop to take a break, let alone pause or, as Davies suggests, stand and stare: 'What is this life if, full of care, we have no time to stand and stare?' (Davis, 1911: online) In this chapter we will discuss the importance of taking time to reflect on professional practice and will consider some of the benefits of doing so. In particular, we will consider the ways in which reflection provides an opportunity to challenge our perspectives and provides scope for deeper learning.

What is reflection and why should we do it?

Reflection is a natural part of our daily lives but can also be something we choose to do deliberately. The process involves an exploration of thoughts and actions and provides the opportunity to evaluate events, so the reasons we may wish to reflect are many. Through reflection we can consider professional values and develop different understandings and approaches. It is also a way of helping us gain insights into the image we project to others. Reflection on professional practice is a positive way of managing change as it provides an opportunity to open our practice up to scrutiny in a way that is safe and in our control.

It can also be a way of sharing our 'stories' (Bolton, 2001) and offers an opportunity to make sense of our experience by co-constructing understanding through discussion with others. However, when we tell and retell our version of events to a range of people, we need to be aware that we may be doing so with a less than critical eye, 'tucking ourselves securely

DOI: 10.4324/9781003056812-2

under a quilt patchworked out of safe and self-affirming accounts (Ibid.: 1). In this way we are expressing a view that is acceptable to us, making comfortable assumptions and reinforcing our current view of the world.

But what if we want to learn from a particular incident? Perhaps we would like to develop our skills in managing a similar experience in the future? For this to happen we need to examine the event from different angles by reviewing our own and others' beliefs about it by 'hunting assumptions' – trying to find out what our assumptions are and testing their validity (Brookfield, 2012: 7).

Through critical reflection we may avoid simplistic cause-and-effect deductions, begin to challenge previously held beliefs and really start to unpick how and why we see things the way we do. Effective reflection, therefore, is something which provides the opportunity not only to tell our stories in ways which allow us to feel secure but also provides a basis from which to critically examine them.

In a professional context, reflective practice also has the important role of challenging hegemony – in this case the dominance of particular beliefs relating to a profession often dictated by powerful influencers such as government departments or professional bodies. Very often these things become so embedded into practice, they are beyond question.

Hegemonic practice in a professional context is informed by what is considered to be 'good' or 'the right way to do things' and is underpinned by technical rationalism (Schön, 1983). In theory this provides a logical approach – which can be attractive to new and experienced practitioners, but it can also result in the application of generic practice, not always applicable in specific contexts. A typical example of this is the accepted practice for teachers to share learning objectives with their students at the beginning of the lesson and then check them regularly throughout the lesson. It is debateable whether or not this actually enhances students' ability to learn but is so embedded it has become a rule of operation. In all professions there are forms of such accepted practice that are so commonplace they are almost sacrosanct.

Such rational practice is often adopted (or adapted) from research or well publicised ideas from powerful others giving it a gravitas which can be difficult to argue with. Research should of course have a place in shaping practice, but we also need to be wary of dualistic thinking, the kind of either/or thought that does not take into account contextual detail.

Even if Heraclitus is right and we live in a state of constant change, there are many good reasons to reflect, not only on professional practice but on life. As people, we may well be different to yesterday and the 'rivers' we step into may be in a state of continual transformation, but there are also transferable aspects to most experiences – and these are the things we can influence. In short, whilst we cannot change the situation, we can certainly change our responses to it. For this reason alone, reflection is a useful and developmental activity, so here are my top ten reasons for doing it.

- Reflection provides a safe forum to be objective and critically analyse our practice.
- It allows us to view things from a range of perspectives.
- It helps us to identify any new skills we may need to develop.
- It helps us to see how others might view us and what impact that might have on professional or personal relationships.

- It helps us to consider how and why we make certain decisions, so that we may choose to make different ones another time.
- It helps us to establish our values.
- It provides a way of analysing areas of difficulty.
- It may help us to manage difficult or painful episodes by looking at them objectively and may be a way of helping us to cope with professional life!
- It can be a strategy for challenging current practice and constructing new learning by identifying other ways of doing things.
- Sharing our reflections with others helps to develop more collegiate approaches.

Weltanschauung

An important consideration within all of this is the influence of *weltanschauung*, which relates to the 'go to' ways in which we interpret aspects of our lives. This is sometimes referred to as 'world view'; although my interpretation of world view is a cognitive process which represents how we have learnt to see things. *Weltanshauung* is more than a philosophy or understanding of the world as it encompasses judgements, perception, ways of thinking, attitudes and norms of behaviour. It can even influence tastes and interests. It may be present at a societal level, represented by a particular culture's judgement of what is good or important, as well as at an individual level, revealed in the values we choose to adopt and the ways in which these influence us. It could be described as a mindset or lens through which we experience and interpret the things directing everyday functioning down to the most mundane details. In this way it influences what we perceive, how we get around in the world and how we relate to other people. As a result, people often see things in very different ways:

> Lillian was bewildered by the enormous discrepancy which existed between Jay's models and what he painted. Together they would walk along the same Seine river, she would see it silky grey, sinuous and glittering, he would draw it opaque with fermented mud, and a shoal of wine bottle corks and weeds caught in the stagnant edges.
>
> (Anais Nin, 1961: 124)

This excerpt taken from Anais Nin's *Seduction of the Minotaur* illustrates this beautifully. Not only do the two characters see things differently, it gives the impression they experience things quite differently and suggests that this accounts for the 'discrepancy' between the artist's models and the way they are depicted. In much the same way, we have all learnt to see things in established ways, which Nin suggests is representative of our sense of being, of who we are: 'We don't see things as they are, we see them as we are'.[1]

The habitual nature of these 'go to' responses suggests that thoughts are governed beyond pure intellect and as such, initial perceptions, understandings or actions are not necessarily foremost in our awareness. This doesn't mean they can't be brought into awareness of course. With a little time, an open mind and a few strategies to prompt us we all have the potential to expand our thinking.

The power of metaphor

Lakoff and Johnson (1980) propose that the way in which we process and interpret informa-tion is largely metaphorical and is evident in the little things we do every day as well as the language we use, and it is by examining language that we may also explore thoughts and actions. As suggested by Winter, 'We do not "store" experience as data, like a computer: we "story" it' (1988: 235). Therefore language and its interpretation is key in developing our depth of understanding and is something which undoubtedly forms part of the reflective process.

5-minute reflection - Downloading

Spend five minutes writing down your thoughts about the day. Do not edit them, just write until the time is up. When you have finished, go back and highlight anything that seems significant in terms of the words you have chosen. Are there any words repeated? Have you focussed on particular aspects of the day? Are there any connec-tions between the two? Do any metaphors fit today's story?

The downloading activity is a strategy for gathering unedited thoughts in order to analyse the language you are using. This provides a clue to the sorts of stories being created about particular events and may offer some nuggets for further reflection. What is particularly useful about this strategy is the process of editing written work - in doing this we really have to think about our choice of words and have the opportunity to analyse our perception of events. It is a starting point to criticality.

It could be argued that the essence of reflection lies within our ability to think critically about what we encounter, and according to Brookfield this is essential if we want to achieve our goals: 'if you can't think critically you will behave in ways that have less chance of achiev-ing the results you want' (2012: 1).

Types of learning

In a professional context, we could argue that 'effective reflection' is that which has an impact on the ways we work. It may offer fresh understandings, greater clarity or a platform for the development of new ideas, and for most people this means that reflection should lead to learning.

For many people when reflecting on the day-to-day problems life throws at us, expressing thoughts and feelings about something is quite a natural process, yet when we transfer this to the workplace the need to find a solution is much more pressing. This means that the focus is often on the problems or unexpected events and we sometimes ignore the 'ordinary', the routine practice or ways of thinking. Such incidents are a good prompt for reflective activity since they are driven by a desire to find a resolution, for example:

Emma views herself as an efficient and supportive manager and is working with a new team of highly skilled and experienced professionals. She has noticed that the team have quite divergent approaches to their work and feels it would be beneficial to everybody if there was more consistency within the department. After reflecting on this concern, Emma decided the solution was to put in place a strong framework of processes and to monitor these regularly. Some members of the team responded well to this . . . others didn't.

Emma was confused by this outcome. In her experience teams run more effectively if there is a general consensus on how to do things. Her belief is that systems should drive practice and without a strong framework, outcomes will be variable. She views consistency as important and after further reflection, Emma decided to reinforce her original ideas and monitor activity more frequently. The original 'compliers' continued to comply, whereas the 'outliers' became even more divergent in their application of the new processes.

In Emma's case, what started out as a straight-forward problem became what Mezirow refers to as a 'disorienting dilemma' (Mezirow, 1991). This is a situation that has arisen which challenges our 'taken for granted' assumptions and is somewhat unsettling. Such a dilemma has the potential to transform practice as it encourages us to reappraise our approaches, understandings and beliefs in a given context. However, for this to be the case, it requires the ability to think about the situation both objectively and critically.

In the example provided, Emma was relying on her tacit knowledge about how to manage a team and was utilising her experience to set up what she thought was an essential requirement for efficient operation. Her dilemma was that not everyone in the team shared this view, and they responded to the changes in divergent ways. By simply reinforcing her original strategy, Emma was not taking a critical approach or showing any willingness to challenge her own assumptions, so in her case the dilemma, whilst disorientating, was not the transformative experience it might have been!

Argyris and Schön (1978: 2) suggest that learning includes the detection and correction of error, which for most people means that when they think something has gone wrong, they look for a strategy to address the issue. In Emma's case, the perceived 'error' is a general lack of consistency in the way her team operates and her solution to this is to set up some formal processes which should (but didn't) lead to a more consistent approach. In Argyris and Schön's view, this is an example of single-loop learning, which often occurs when the emphasis is on techniques and their effectiveness. It could be described as pragmatic in that a problem is explored and a potential solution is found but when the 'solution' does not work as expected, it can lead to a sense of being stuck. The example often used to explain this theory is that of a thermostat which has one automatic and limited type of reaction – when it detects a room is too cold, it switches on, when it detects that the room is too hot, it switches off. There is little insight needed.

This can be translated into organisational behaviour where inflexible procedures are established and the focus is on detecting and adjusting any deviations from the 'rules' rather than revaluating the core framework and the assumptions upon which it was developed. In most cases procedures are established based on a solution-focussed approach, so there is a certain logic in ensuring that they are followed. They may even be based on research evidence and as such also have the added kudos of being somewhat 'scientific'. Compliance with established norms of practice is a less risky approach for individuals as they can presuppose that the processes they follow were set up for good reason and for the organisation, such compliance affords greater control, therefore 'rule makers' and 'rule takers' are often complicit in maintaining the status quo. But in a rapidly changing society, is this the best approach? Is there also a danger in not critically evaluating our practice?

An alternative is double-loop learning, which occurs when a problem is identified and the solution requires a critical appraisal of current norms of practice. This means we may question our original hypothesis and its underlying assumptions and in doing so may change our approach to a particular task and even question the task itself. Double-loop learning has the potential to be transformational as it offers a different perspective and a range of options. Figure 1.1 outlines this model in relation to Emma's story.

We are not always in a position to change or influence practice at an organisational level, so at times our reflection may simply be about understanding an event and thinking about what we need to do to resolve a particular situation. For this a good starting point is the What? So What? Now What? Approach (Rolfe *et al.*, 2001). This involves three simple stages:

What? - outlines the event or problem and considers:

- What was my aim in this event?
- What was my role?
- What actions did I take?
- What responses did I get?
- What were the consequences?
- What was good/bad about the experience?

So what? - explores the meaning of the experience:

- What was the thinking behind this?
- What does this tell me about my actions/attitudes?
- What does this imply about my relationships with others?
- What other knowledge can I bring to the situation? (for example, literature/others' views)

Now what? - considers actions to move forwards:

- What do I need to do to resolve this?
- What broader issues should be considered?
- What might be the consequences of planned actions?

In the case of Emma's disorientating dilemma, is it possible that by adopting a simple model of reflection some clarity might be offered to the situation? The what? element of the model is clearly outlined in the account on the previous pages (Emma tried and failed to implement

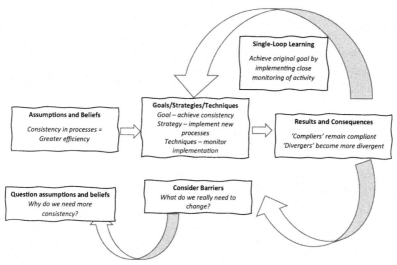

Figure 1.2 Single- and double-loop learning
Source: Adapted from Argyris & Schön, 1978

consistent processes) but how could Emma employ the rest of the model in a way that might provide new understandings and potential actions? Reflecting on the proposed questions has the potential to offer greater insights. At the very least it prompts more balanced thought. Simply asking 'What does this tell me about my actions/attitudes?' offers up the idea that interactions involve more than one person and that all participants have a part to play in the outcome; and by asking 'What other knowledge can I bring to the situation?' we are acknowledging that we do not need to have all the answers and that others may be able to offer some useful insights.

10-Minute Reflection - What/So what/Now what?

Think back over the last week and pick out an event that has troubled you. It doesn't have to be a big event, just something that prompted you to think a little more than usual. Using the structure and questions outlined in the What? So What? Now What? Approach, explore the event in a little more detail.

Reflection, perception and interpretation

The examples used in this chapter have been shared to illustrate the ways in which perception can influence what we see and believe. In many ways, this seems like an obvious statement, but we are continually presented with examples that suggest a general feeling that our own perception is in fact truth!

Truth is most often associated with reality and authenticity. In our professional lives, truth is based on our training and the tacit knowledge developed through professional experience. Our learning and experiences shape who we are and what we believe, and in the process of professional development we not only gather knowledge and skills but also a range of attitudes and beliefs which certainly have an influence on what is 'true' for us.

Reflecting on these truths presents us with a number of challenges. As humans we interpret ourselves as products of our own personal and professional backgrounds, but this interpretation is influenced by the very background we are trying to view objectively. Just think about all the inculcated messages received from family, friends, education, workplace and you have an inkling of the potential number of influencing factors. Hence, we don't necessarily see things as they are, we see them as we are.

In a sense any interpretation is as an 'insider' in a context which we are aiming to view from the 'outside', therefore the context itself must be interpreted if we are to critically analyse events. New understandings are produced through a systematic analysis which includes attention to the conditions and environment in which we are entrenched.

A key aim of reflection is to help us make sense of our practice. This doesn't always mean getting direct answers to questions or solutions to problems, nor does it mean that we are necessarily in control of events. Paradoxically, one way to improve reflection might be to let go of the need to make complete sense of something or to immediately find a solution to a problem. Learning may come about in a more circuitous way and can involve occupying a sometimes uncomfortable space of 'not knowing'. As Rogers said all those years ago: 'The only person who is educated is the person who has learned how to learn: the person who has learned how to adapt and change; the person who has realised that no knowledge gives a basis for security' (Rogers, 1969: 152). Like the example of double-loop learning (Argyris & Schön, 1978) this means questioning assumptions and beliefs whilst taking into account potential barriers to change. It may mean ignoring the search for a solution because we have redefined the problem.

Chapter reflections

In this chapter we have explored the role of reflection in enhancing personal and professional development and considered the importance of perception in influencing what we see, believe and do. Taking account of the importance of criticality, hunting out assumptions and analysing the stories we present to others, we have begun to lay the foundations for reflective practice.

Note

1   Anais Nin accredits this saying to the Babylonian Talmud

References

Argyris, C., & Schön, D. (1978) *Organizational Learning: A Theory of Action Perspective*. Reading, MA: Addison Wesley.

Bolton, G. (2001) *Reflective Practice, Writing and Professional Development*. London: Paul Chapman Publishing Ltd.

Brookfield, S. D. (2012) *Teaching for Critical Thinking, Tools and Techniques to Help Students Question their Assumptions*. San Francisco, CA: Jossey-Bass.

Davis, W. H. (1911) 'Leisure'. Available at: https://englishverse.com/poems/leisure [date accessed: 20/1/21].

Khan, C. H. (1979) *The Art and Thought of Heraclitus, an Edition of the Fragments with Translation and Commentary*. Cambridge: Cambridge University Press.

Lakoff, G., & Johnson, M. (1980) *Metaphors We Live By*. Chicago: University of Chicago Press.

Mezirow, J. (1991) *Transformative Dimensions of Adult Learning*. San Francisco, CA: Jossey-Bass.

Nin, A. (1961) *Seduction of the Minotaur*. Chicago: The Swallow Press.

Rogers, C. (1969) *Freedom to Learn: A View of What Education Might Become*. Columbus: Charles. E. Merrill.

Rolfe, G., Freshwater, D., & Jasper, M. (2001) *Critical Reflection in Nursing and the Helping Professions: A User's Guide*. Basingstoke: Palgrave Macmillan.

Schön, D. A. (1983) *The Reflective Practitioner: How Professionals Think in Action*. New York, NY: Basic Books.

Winter, R. (1988) 'Fictional-Critical Writing'. In J. Nias & S. Groundwater-Smith (eds.), *The Enquiring Teacher*. London: Falmer, pp. 231–248.

Figure 2.1 Chapter mindmap

2 Learning through practice

Learning is something we tend to take for granted without thinking much about how we learn or even defining what it means to have learnt something. Some definitions of learning refer to the acquisition of knowledge and skills, others to a process closely connected to how we gather information from our environment. Learning appears to have become quite popularised, certainly in terms of our use of the word; we live in a 'learning age' driven by an aspiration to build human capital through the continued acquisition of knowledge and skills . . . in theory at least! Through a process of 'learnification' or the new language of learning, (Biesta, 2009) we are now quite likely to refer to learner autonomy, learning profiles, learning technologies and learning environments. Yet despite popular usage of the word, clarity around what learning is seems to be elusive: 'Questions about learning are addressed in virtually all areas of psychology. It is therefore surprising to see that researchers are rarely explicit about what they mean by the term' (De Houwer et al., 2013 online). In this chapter we will reflect on types of learning which are pertinent to professional practice and within this will explore the meaning of situated learning and the ways in which communities of practice can help to develop our thinking and our expertise.

Learning is an individual and very complex process; it is usually something we do without thinking about it too much and as a result can be difficult to define. Recent research around the topic suggests that very little learning actually comes through deliberate teaching but has more to do with participation in life: 'Children learn by watching and imitating the people around them (observational learning) and they learn by listening to what other people say about how the world works – 'learning from testimony' (Gopnik, 2016: 89).

Learning has also been viewed as transformation, but for this to be the case we need to actively challenge current thinking. According to Mezirow we all have certain 'frames of reference' that shape the way we understand things. These have the useful function of providing structure to our understanding within which we can slot new learning. Frames of reference are not necessarily based on accepted facts, they may be attached to supposition and as Dewey suggests: 'insinuate themselves into acceptance and become unconsciously a part of our mental furniture' (1910: 5). They can be limiting as well as useful, so the importance of being critically aware of what and how we are thinking will allow us to 'extend our understanding and make alternative choices' (Mezirow, 1997: 167). Learning as transformation

DOI: 10.4324/9781003056812-3

requires perspective change or at the very least a stretching of the frames within which we contain knowledge.

Situated learning

Within our culture, it is easy to assume that learning takes place supported by the architecture of formal systems of education. We learn at school, college and university. Within these frameworks, learning is placed into a given curriculum model, has a clear beginning and end and has a recognisable outcome which is usually dependent on teaching and testing. Most curricula and classrooms are designed on the basis of these assumptions designating learning as a specialised activity which is contained within a protected environment and one which is very much separate from other parts of our lives.

Unlike traditional, classroom-based learning, situated learning occurs within its natural environment, for example we learn how to communicate from our families, we learn about a new job from our colleagues and we absorb cultural learning through interactions that are common within social settings. In contrast to classroom-based learning, which is usually out of context and somewhat abstract, situated learning is of the present moment and firmly placed within the environment in which it takes place. In this sense, learning is not seen as a formal acquisition of knowledge but as the result of participation in social interaction and collaboration - it is a part of our lived experience (Wenger, 2000).

Lave and Wenger (1991) use the term 'community of practice' to describe the ways in which learning takes place through social interaction in communities of common interest and collaboration. Communities of practice provide an opportunity for members to collaborate through the sharing of knowledge and resources, as well as acting as a forum for discussing ideas. We all belong to communities of practice at home or at work and sometimes through our personal interests. They are an integral part of daily life, but in a professional context they take on a more structured form and are normally facilitated by professional bodies whose aim is to promote collaboration in order to develop expertise within the field. Learning within communities of practice is an outcome of social participation, and when we become active participants we have a forum for developing our understanding and enhancing what we do (Wenger, 2000).

Situated learning and learning by doing

Situated learning is by its nature experiential and is based on a close connection between activity, involvement and problem solving within a community of practice. It is distinctly different to 'learning by doing', which could be achieved by building a practical activity into a learning context and is very often something contrived as part of the teaching process. A teacher demonstrating how to do something and then guiding students to do the same for themselves is an example of learning by doing. This may or may not involve social participation within the group, but it does involve an active approach to skill development.

Situated learning goes beyond the acquisition of certain forms of knowledge and is actively placed within social relationships. More specifically it is positioned in situations designed for co-participation in authentic contexts of practice. So rather than focussing on the cognitive processes involved in the learning, the question is 'What type of social engagement is required for learning to take place?'

How to make communities of practice work for you

Being invited to participate in a community of practice is an exciting opportunity providing a dedicated space for personal or professional development. Such communities exist within a range of disciplines and may take place within organisations or externally in the wider professional sphere – they may even take place at an international level. There are a number of professional associations whose aim is to develop networks of practitioners who collaborate in the sharing and advancing of knowledge in their field. These communities also have an additional role, that of elevating the status of the profession overall as they have an important function in maintaining and enhancing the esteem with which a particular profession is held.

Most networks are now supported by technology, which means that it is easy to communicate with others and participate in regular training events. Online portals also offer access to vast amounts of knowledge and ideas are generated through websites, blogs and discussion boards. For someone who wants to develop their knowledge and skills within a particular field this seems like a Utopian ideal. However, as with many things, getting started isn't always a simple process. Within my own field there are many communities of practice which have the potential to offer developmental opportunities, but experience has taught me to be selective, firstly because of time limitations and secondly because not all communities are developmental. For this reason alone it is worth spending time thinking about where your interests really lie and then considering what you want to get out of participating in a particular community. Once you start looking for groups a lot of pathways open up and eventually turn into a maze!

Create a list of your areas of professional interest. Then search for networks active in these fields and talk to your colleagues about any groups they participate in.
My list would look something like this:

- Teaching and Learning effectiveness
- Professional agency
- Professional development

Each of those areas has relevant groups and a variety of forums including Twitter, special interest groups, usually linked to research associations such as BERA (British Association of Research in Education) and professional bodies like the Chartered College of Teaching. All of them have websites or blogs and most have meetings or conferences where members can get together.

One factor to consider is that many professional bodies require members to pay a fee and if you join more than one this can become costly, so it is important to find what works for you. You could take the trial-and-error approach – I simply created a list of all my interests and tested which were a good fit. This may seem a little long-winded, but it did provide the impetus to explore a range of options – essential when you don't really know what you are looking for! Sometimes it takes a while to get to the right answer and sometimes we don't always know the extent of the search, but the exploration can be an adventure that may lead to interesting discoveries: 'An explorer can never know what he is exploring until it is explored' (Bateson, 2000: xxiv).

In order to make communities of practice work for you there are a few things to consider:

- The knowledge contained within the community – is there a particular focus or is the community open to new ideas and developments? Some groups, such as professional bodies, have a very strong focus in terms of maintaining and enhancing practice; others, such as discussion groups, have more of a focus on idea generation.
- The way the community operates – how formal is the structure? How and where do members meet? Is there a cost associated with joining? Many interest groups are free and often discussion is web-based or based on meetings of small groups, whereas most professional bodies have a formalised structure, charge a membership fee and tend to organise larger events such as annual conferences.
- Methods of participation – are there open discussion forums or more formalised channels of communication? Does the group have a journal or blog? Is this open access and can you share your own expertise using these vehicles?

The most important thing in all of this of course is the benefits of participation in the community, more specifically, how this might inform reflection and in turn improve practice.

Deliberate practice

Whilst the focus of this book is on reflection and how to get the most out of developing this habit, it is worth mentioning that we normally reflect for a purpose. This might be to gain a more in-depth understanding of something, but it also has a more practical outcome in that it helps to develop our overall expertise.

When we consider what it is to be expert it is easy to attribute specific skills with natural talents, much in the same way as we would for an artist or musician – describing them as 'gifted', suggesting that their talent was simply handed over to them. But what of more ordinary mortals? Are we destined to mediocrity because we have not been gifted a specific set of skills and abilities? Of course not! In exactly the same way as most gifted creators are not simply given their abilities – most of them have had to work at it. In fact, some researchers ascribe expertise to a more structured activity, that of deliberate practice (Ericsson *et al.*, 1993).

You may have come across the 10,000-hour rule (Gladwell, 2009) which put forward the idea that it takes around 10,000 hours of practice to develop expertise in a particular domain. This idea was based on the research of Erikson *et al.*, but what was taken from it was the simple statistic – that it requires 10,000 hours of practice to become expert at something. This does not take into account the important aspects of deliberate practice, i.e., practice as a structured activity the involves the mastery of a specific skillset. We could of course spend 10,000 hours practising things that do nothing to develop our expertise, whereas for deliberate practice we would need to consider:

- The fundamentals to be mastered – all skills require a number of small actions that build on each other, and we are unlikely to be able to master them all at once, but we can work on one small component at a time. For example, when learning to play the piano we must learn individual keys before we can master chords.
- The next aim would be to master the small steps – this is where the practice comes in. Dedicated practice and repetition until actions become more fluent. One small component would be mastered before moving to the next.
- Finally, to ensure that we are practising the right things in the right way – get feedback from an expert. This not only provides confirmation when we are getting it right but also guidance if some aspect of performance needs to be developed.

By reflecting on our professional expertise and working in collaboration through communities of practice, it is possible to take very deliberate steps to developing your expertise – and this won't necessarily take 10,000 hours!

Critical incidents

A first step in developing expertise is highlighting those areas in which we feel confident and those where we do not – for whatever reason. This may be due to gaps in knowledge or simply that we have not had the opportunity to enhance a particular aspect of our work. It can be difficult to know where to start and the early days of reflection may be presented as a random collection of thoughts. That's fine, as the first step is to start and to establish a habit of reflecting. It is perfectly acceptable to write anything and everything, but as time progresses you will find that you cultivate a certain style within your reflection and you are likely to see patterns both in terms of what you are reflecting on and in how you are structuring your thoughts.

A critical incident is an event which for one or more reasons has special significance. It is something that we interpret as a problem or challenge in a particular context rather than a routine occurrence. The majority of critical incidents are not at all dramatic or obvious and for other people may not be considered critical – they are often very commonplace events but become critical when they are indicative of underlying trends or structures. Critical incidents are personal to each of us and, whilst at a superficial level they might appear to represent typical events, they are rendered critical through analysis (Tripp, 2011).

Take a look at these two events and decide whether or not you would consider them critical incidents worthy of reflection.

This description is based on a mentor's observation of a lesson with Adam, who is a Trainee Teacher.

Adam is well organised and has planned well for his lesson. He has developed a lot of useful resources for the class and has the learners working in small groups actively involved in a range of activities. This necessitates their moving from the existing seat-ing arrangement and collecting exercise books and resources. Initially this works well, but then the noise levels begin to rise and there is a haphazard claiming of books and resources. Learners begin to shout above one another in order to be heard, and Adam's response is to quell the class by shouting at them.

The initial response from the group is to go about collecting materials with less noise but then the noise levels begin to creep up again. When he notices this, Adam begins to make threats, which the learners appear to ignore. They settle noisily into their groups and work through the task with mixed application. There are many inter-ruptions, some of them unnecessary, and Adam is occupied responding to individual pockets of disruption.

The time for break arrives before Adam has the opportunity to prepare for the ple-nary. The learners draw his attention to the break time, and he disperses them. They leave in a somewhat disorderly way.

This is an excerpt from a Trainee's reflective diary:

I had to teach a lesson on the use of statistics in business . . . something I don't know much about and find really dull. I spent all night preparing for it, constantly going over and over the material in order to ensure that I fully understood it. I made up a lot of activities – to help the students but really to keep them occupied so that they didn't ask me too many difficult questions. I was dreading the lesson . . . but guess what? It went really well. I feel I can relax now . . . well at least until the next time I have to teach this.

Did you consider these to be critical incidents? In most cases people recognise the first as somewhat critical – a trainee teacher who feels the way to manage behaviour is to shout and threaten probably isn't going to survive well in today's classroom. It is easy to see why this might be considered something worthy of reflection so that alternative strategies could be generated. But what of the second reflection? This account is of something which caused anxiety but turned out to be successful? Would this be considered a critical incident? When we consider standard definitions of critical incidents, we tend to think of events out of the range of normal experience that involve a threat to life or at the very least present a strong threat to the status quo. However, in a professional context a critical incident can be defined as something which, for whatever reason, appears significant to us. It will usually be some-thing that we are drawn to thinking about. Although the second example was a successful event, it was something that had caused anxiety, which is certainly worth reflection, and there was a surprising discovery – again, a reflection-worthy event.

Another way to consider critical incidents is something that taps into the interaction sys-tems of our emotions. There are three of these to think about (Butler *et al.*, 2018):

- Threat system – linked to anxiety and anger, often leading to seeking safety or self-protection.

- Drive system - associated with excitement and vitality. This is what helps us to pursue goals and achievements.
- Soothing system - linked to warmth, connectedness and contentment.

An incident which could be considered critical would bring about some emotion linked to these systems. In the example of Adam there was most certainly a threat in a situation that could get out of control and the second incident caused some excitement with the potential to drive the writer towards finding some element of transferable learning from the event.

Critical incidents are a very good starting point for reflection as they have already prompted a response in us. They may be troubling, exciting, scary . . . or simply interesting – but how do we know when we have come across one?

10-Minute Reflection - Video replay

This activity requires you to be in a relaxed state, so it may be best to start with a few deep breaths or a yoga move or two - whatever does the trick for you! Once relaxed, re-run the events of the week through your mind as if you are watching a video replay of them. As you do this, notice any tensions or positive feelings. Just go with it, no judgement or analysis. Simply let the video play out. When you have finished, jot down notes of the most vivid images and note any emotions that were apparent during the replay.

The video replay activity is an opportunity to review experiences objectively - like an outsider looking in - and provides the opportunity to focus on things in more detail. With practice you can even do this in slow motion, offering the scope to notice details you may have missed in real time. Taking into account that our memories are not foolproof and that perception will influence what we see, this is a useful activity as it is likely to reveal much about the feelings attached to certain events, and anything which prompts a reaction is usually a good source for reflection.

Recording your reflection

When you start your reflective journey, one thing you will need to consider is how you will record your reflections. Whilst it is possible to keep information in your head, it isn't advisable if you wish to explore patterns, find links and synthesise your thoughts. In addition, the practice of recording reflections can be a cathartic process. Traditionally reflection has taken the form of writing, usually in a journal, however other methods can be employed depending on your preferences, for example mindmaps, images or voice recordings and of course journals, which do not need to be the traditional handwritten, hardback documents many of us recognise. There are lots of online tools and apps you can employ. If you are happy to share your reflections, you might also want to record them in a blog or a Vlog. It is worth experimenting with a number of things to find what works well for you. If you have carried out the 5- or 10-minute reflection strategies introduced so far, you may find you already have a good start to developing your reflective practice and can test out one or two methods of recording reflections.

Chapter reflections

In this chapter we have considered the links between reflection and learning with a particular focus on forms of situated learning. Much reflective activity is based on our experiences and the ways in which we make meaning from them – in particular, those experiences which prompt emotional responses. Having a greater awareness of our feelings, actions and reactions in turn helps us to have more control over these aspects of our practice. It isn't a guaranteed fix for the things that don't serve us but is most certainly a step in the right direction.

References

Bateson, G. (2000) *Steps to an Ecology of Mind*. Chicago: University of Chicago Press.
Biesta, G. J. J. (2009) 'Good Education in An Age of Measurement: On the Need to Reconnect with the Question of Purpose in Education'. *Educational Assessment, Evaluation and Accountability*, 21(1): 33–46.
Butler, G., Grey, N., & Hope, T. (2018) *Managing Your Mind – The Mental Fitness Guide* (3rd ed.). Oxford: Oxford University Press.
De Houwer, J., Barnes-Holmes, D., & Moors, A. (2013) 'What Is Learning? On the Nature and Merits of a Functional Definition of Learning'. *Psychonomic Bulletin & Review*. doi: 10.3758/s13423-013-0386-3. Available at: https://ppw.kuleuven.be/okp/_pdf/DeHouwer2013WILOT.pdf [date accessed: 8/6/18].
Dewey, J. (1910) *How We Think*. Boston, MA: D. C. Heath & Co.
Ericsson, K. A., Krampe, R. T., & Tesch-Romer, C. (1993) 'The Role of Deliberate Practice in the Acquisition of Expert Performance'. *Psychological Review*, 100(3): 363–406.
Gladwell, M. (2009) *Outliers the Story of Success*. London: Penguin Books.
Gopnik, A. (2016) *The Carpenter and the Gardener. What the New Science of Child Development Tells Us about the Relationship Between Parents and Children*. London: Boadley Head.
Lave, J., & Wenger, E. (1991) *Situated Learning: Legitimate Peripheral Participation*. Cambridge: Cambridge University Press.
Mezirow, J. (1997) *Transformative Dimensions of Adult Learning*. San Francisco, CA: Jossey-Bass.
Tripp, D. (2011) *Critical Incidents in Teaching – Developing Professional Judgement*. Oxon: Routledge.
Wenger, E. (2000) *Communities of Practice, Learning, Meaning and Identity*. Cambridge: Cambridge University Press.

Figure 3.1 Chapter mindmap

3 Models of reflection

As outlined in previous chapters, acquiring the habit of reflection provides a platform to examine and learn from experiences in ways that develop new insights about ourselves and how we work. Through honest reflection we are able to develop a level of self-awareness that allows us to critically examine our assumptions about and responses to events, and by adding structure to our reflections we increase the ability to think about them objectively. This seems like a simple enhancement to practice, but for anyone in a professional context it is so much more than that. Learning to reflect openly and honestly is not just the icing on the cake, it is a key ingredient in the mix for any professional role. In this chapter we are going to consider several ways of structuring reflections by exploring some popular models of reflection.

Reflection can be any activity that causes us to think about experiences in ways that encourage questions, new thoughts and potential actions, which in turn could lead to changes in perspectives or behaviour. Our experience forms the basis of the knowledge we gather as our expertise grows, and as outlined in chapter two, much of this stems from situated learning. Through this process we create tacit knowledge, not from being taught but from personal experience developed over time, and like other forms of knowledge what we 'know' should sometimes be brought into question to ensure that we continue to build on it. In this way, reflection can not only become an enhancement to practice, it can transform it. In today's rapid-paced society, this ability is essential to allow us to adapt to and welcome change. As I write this, we are experiencing the COVID-19 pandemic. which has impacted on every aspect of society across the world. Not only are we changing our day-to-day activities, we must also embrace different ways of working and being. I suspect many people are reflecting on their lives as a result, but should we need a life-threatening scenario to create the space for this endeavour?

In the well-loved book *Winnie the Pooh*, there is a passage describing how Edward Bear, bumps his head on the stairs as Christopher Robin drags him along: 'It is, as far as he knows, the only way of coming downstairs, but sometimes he feels there really is another way. If only he could stop bumping for a moment and think of it' (Milne, 1926: 1). Most of us spend our days 'bumping' along without questioning what we are doing or how we are doing it, perhaps because of the power of routine or because we feel we don't have the space to think about

DOI: 10.4324/9781003056812-4

how we might do things differently. It is possible that we have been doing what we do in the way that we do it for so long we may not know where to start. We may also be influenced by the communities we work in, by colleagues, managers and organisation processes, all of which serve to 'drag' us along in much the same way as the bear's journey down the stairs. In my research into learning spaces for teachers (Thompson & Wolstencroft, 2018) many of the participants made reference to the limitations placed on them by organisational processes and the need for conformity around how the professional role was enacted. For these partici- pants, what they viewed as controlling factors, (usually *diktats* about how to teach) shaped a diminished sense of professional identity which not only impacted on their ability to be crea- tive but also their willingness to take charge of the professional role. They no longer took the time to reflect on their practice because they didn't see the point!

Models of reflective practice

If we are to learn from our experiences, finding time for reflection is the first step towards creating positive change and exploring a range of ways in which we can do this is a useful starting point. Whilst I don't necessarily advocate sticking rigidly to a particular approach, I am aware that it can sometimes be difficult to begin the process, so using a model becomes a useful framework. The problem is, there are so many to choose from it is difficult to know where to start. Figure 3.2 outlines a range of popular models of reflection and the key prin- ciples common to most of them. It is intended as a summary to highlight the similarities and differences between them. Information on any of these models is readily available if you would like to explore them further, and some of them have been outlined in more detail in this chapter.

Gibbs' reflective cycle

A popular model for reflective practice is Gibbs' Cycle (1998), which includes six stages and is outlined in Figure 3.3. The aim of the model is to challenge current practice through evalua- tion and analysis, which should in turn lead to potential actions. The focus is on learning from experiences by analysing them objectively. Working through the cycle may involve asking yourself several questions such as:

- What happened, where and when? (the specific details of the event)
- What did I/others do?
- How did I feel during and after the experience?
- How did the experience begin and end?
- What went well/what could have been better?
- What was the outcome?
- Are there any connections with other experiences?
- What else could I have done?
- What does this mean for my practice?
- What could I try next time this happens?

Atkins and Murphy Cycle (1993) - avoid superficial responses to events. Includes the following stages:

- Awareness
- Description of situation
- Analysis of feelings and knowledge
- Evaluation of relevance
- Identification of learning

Boud et al. Triangular Representation (1985) highlights the link between reflection and learning and contains 3 simple stages:

- Experience
- Reflection
- Learning.

ERA Cycle (Jasper 2013) like Boud et al. considers three stages to reflection:

- Experience
- Reflection
- Action

Gibbs Reflective Cycle (1998) A cycle approach which contains 6 stages:

- Description
- Feelings
- Evaluation
- Analysis
- Conclusion
- Action plan

Some key principles in these models:

Reflection usually relates to an experience

Raises awareness of events

Provides the opportunity to view different perspectives

May involve acknowledging and examining feelings

Makes sense of experiences

May lead to further investigation and learning

Increases self-awareness

Provides a basis for change

Considers alternative actions

Brookfield's Lenses (20) 17 Analyses a situation using 4 different lenses:

- Self (how do I view the situation?)
- Students (how might students see this?)
- Peers (what might my colleagues think of this?)
- Theoretical perspective (what does the literature say?)

Through the Looking Glass (Bolton 2001) focusses on reflexivity and is based on 3 foundations:

- Certain uncertainty
- Serious playfulness
- Unquestioning questioning

Has a focus on trust in the reflective process/ Socratic approach to questioning.

John's (2000) Model of Structured Reflection includes:

- Aesthetics (the art of what we do)
- Personal (self-awareness)
- Ethics (moral knowledge)
- Empirics (scientific knowledge)

Also considers reflexivity, taking into account connections with previous experience.

Kolb's Experiential Learning Cycle (1984) includes:

- Concrete experience (what happened)
- Reflection observations (reflections on events)
- Abstract conceptualisation (what does it mean?)
- Active experimentation (what else could I do?)

Mezirow Transformative Learning (1997) - This model is based on the practice of critically evaluating assumptions -'frames of reference' which inform viewpoints and introduced the notion of disorientating dilemmas, events which may prompt a change in our frames of reference. This model includes experience, deep reflection, questioning and reviewing.

Schön Reflection in action – Reflection on action (1991) – reflection that happens during an event (reflection in action) considering the experience itself and deciding how to act, and reflection that happens after an event (reflection on action) – consideration theoretical perspectives and what you might do differently next time.

Figure 3.2 Models of reflection

Figure 3.3 Gibb's model

This is sometimes described as an iterative model, which means learning through repetition. For this reason the cycle element is important – we are not simply analysing an experience but are considering how it might by altered by changing aspects of it. This means actively seeking out opportunities to revisit experiences so that you can approach them in a different way. It also requires an investment in trying out new strategies which may then be reflected upon and adapted as many times as we feel necessary. This is a good strategy for events that form a regular part of your day-to-day activities but may be less useful for one-off episodes.

In a nutshell – this is an iterative model based on a cycle. The practitioner is prompted by questions which lead them through the process of recording and analysing an event in order to consider what they might do differently should a similar situation occur in the future.

Brookfield's lenses

An alternative model is offered by Brookfield (2017), who suggests that reflection is enhanced by applying critical 'lenses' through which we view things. The premise of this model is to uncover our assumptions by reflecting from alternative perspectives so that we are not viewing something from a singular standpoint. As Brookfield suggests, we are all 'trapped' within the frameworks we are familiar with and: 'A self-confirming cycle often develops in which our assumptions shape our actions that are then interpreted to find the truth of those assumptions' (page 61). Whilst this may be a somewhat comforting scenario as we are almost certainly going to have our beliefs about our experiences validated, it is unlikely to be transformative in terms of a learning experience.

The four lenses model considers the following viewpoints:

- Autobiographical lens
- Students' views
- Colleagues' views
- Theoretical lens

The autobiographical lens is a self-reflection and relates to personal experiences both as a teacher and as a learner. This is an important source of insight as it offers experiences we have felt at a visceral level (as a learner) and encourages reflection on why we have adopted certain strategies as a teacher. This will certainly have a powerful impact on our interpretation and provides us with access to a range of knowledge that we are unlikely to gain from other perspectives. However, basing our reflections purely on experiential insights might be dismissed as somewhat anecdotal. We have not gathered any empirical data and our beliefs and assumptions will most certainly influence our thought processes.

The students' view may well offer some unexpected and useful information. By looking at a scenario in this way we learn how our actions are interpreted by others. Things we may have said or done almost without thinking can sometimes have a profound effect on those within our sphere of influence, and gathering this information has the potential to lead to responsive teaching. This lens is based on the principle that seeing ourselves through learners' eyes offers a valid source of feedback for our practice. Whilst the student's view can be gained from reflecting on your own experiences as a learner it can also be based on gathering actual feedback. If this is the case, an important point to consider is the issue of power within relationships. Teachers are in a privileged position in that they have the power to pass, fail, or assign a grade to a piece of work, and inevitably this knowledge may influence how honest students feel they can be. There are a range of strategies that can be used, from very informal 'post-it' tasks (where you might ask 'what did you find most helpful in this lesson?' and 'what was least helpful?') or mobile technology (for example, mobile voting tools such as Mentimeter) to more formal approaches such as end-of-unit surveys. A key consideration is finding a strategy in which others will feel they are able to offer constructive and honest feedback.

Colleagues offer a useful perspective on our practice in that they are objective observers to our habits and behaviours. In addition, they are able to share their own experiences and may help us to formulate workable solutions to the problems we encounter. Participating in critical reflection with our peers is a way of prompting questions as well as options for alternative action. It is essentially a forum for honest and open dialogue, as Brookfield states:

'Talking to our colleagues about what we do unravels the shroud of silence in which our practice is wrapped' (1998: 200).

The theoretical lens has a dual purpose - it allows us to normalise what may seem like idiosyncratic experiences and offers a range of perspectives from which to analyse them. Applying ideas from theory to your practice can be both disappointing and liberating. Disappointment arises when we discover that our 'unique' experiences have a 'textbook' feel about them but dissipates when we realise that we are not necessarily responsible for everything that happens in our professional context. There is also the potential to generate new ideas for practice by reading and analysing other people's thoughts on it.

In a nutshell - this model provides the opportunity to view something from a range of perspectives. Taking this approach provides scope to challenge individual assumptions and consider different approaches.

Johns' model of structured reflection (2000)

This model was originally designed for a healthcare setting and is focussed on two aspects - 'looking in,' which involves identifying thoughts and emotions, and 'looking out,' which is a description of an event. The framework of the model comes from Carper's 'Ways of Knowing' - a typology classifying four different sources of knowledge (Empirical, Personal, Ethical and Aesthetic) (Carper, 1978).

Empirical knowledge is gathered via observation and experimentation. This is the sort of information taken from research: objective 'facts' which are systematically organised into general theories or laws. It is often linked the knowledge we might gather whilst undertaking professional training. For teachers this might be the learning theories which influence classroom practice. For doctors it could relate to scientific research linked to case histories. When reflecting we might employ empirical knowledge by asking:

- What do I know about this situation?
- What knowledge could have informed me?'

Personal knowledge relates to what we have learnt from the things we have seen and experienced. It is the tacit knowledge based on a cumulation of observation, reflection and practice and is usually acquired over a period of time. Personal knowledge is less fact-based than empirical knowledge in that it has more of an intuitive base (albeit based on experience). In this case you might ask yourself:

- How do I feel about this situation?
- How were others feeling?

Ethical knowing is connected to our moral code, the sense of knowing what is right and wrong, and you might ask yourself:

- Am I acting for the best?
- Have I followed ethical guidelines?

Aesthetic knowing links to a practitioner's individual response to a situation rather than the more stereotyped approach that might result from following the rules or laws set out by empirical evidence. It involves perceiving or grasping the nature of a given situation, using learning from past experience but not necessarily acting in the same way. In a sense it is what makes your professional practice an 'art' by tapping into more intuitive responses and might lead to the questions:

- What am I trying to achieve?
- What are the potential consequences?

In a later version of the model Johns (2017) developed an 'influencers grid' outlining some factors which could be considered to gain insight into responses. This prompts consideration of:

- Expectations from others in relation to 'How I should act?', taking into account habit, conforming to accepted practice and fear of sanction (If I don't conform).
- Expectations from self about 'How I should act?', which considers beliefs, assumptions, values and ethics.
- Factors which influenced my response, including knowledge, past experience, lack of support/resources, time and priorities.

An important consideration in this model is that of critical self-reflection, sometimes referred to as reflexivity: 'finding strategies for looking at our own though processes, values, prejudices and habitual action, as if we were onlookers' (Bolton, 2010: 7).

In a nutshell – this model considers different types of knowledge and how they might influence thoughts and actions. Using question prompts, it provides a structured approach to analysing a situation in order to gain a deeper understanding of it.

A Note about Reflexivity

The terms 'reflective practice' and 'reflexivity' are often used interchangeably, which can cause a little confusion. Reflective practice is simply a process used to enable learning from experience. As suggested by Dewey it goes beyond the random, inconsequential thoughts that simply run through our heads and involves a more sequential approach in which thoughts develop each other:

> Reflection involves not simply a sequence of ideas, but a consequence – a consecutive ordering in such a way that each determines the next as its proper outcome, while each in turn leans back on its predecessors. The successive portions of the reflective thought grow out of one another and support one another; they do not come and go in a medley.

(Dewey, 1910: 2–3) Reflexivity refers to the relationship between cause and effect, especially when linked to our belief structures, so it involves an examination of our beliefs, judgements and subsequent actions. In essence, being reflexive means we are paying close attention to our own thoughts, feelings and the things we do as well as the effects they may have, whereas being reflective is thinking about the whole scenario without this specific focus.

Through the looking glass

In Carroll's *Through the Looking-Glass, and What Alice Found There* (1871) Alice enters a strange world in which everything is reversed. This rule wasn't limited to things she saw but was also applied to logic, and she discovered that running kept her stationary and to go towards something she had to move away from it. Familiar things became very different. Because of this she could take nothing for granted and had to learn not only to do things differently but how to think in different ways.

A reflection in a mirror provides us with an identical (albeit reversed) image which is likely to represent current and accepted narratives – we are seeing things the way that we 'know' they are, but if we are to take a reflexive approach, the value of acknowledging different perspectives and challenging current narratives becomes much more important. A 'through the mirror' approach is based on the idea of making the familiar strange in much the same way as in Alice's adventures. Bolton (2001) suggests that there are three foundations for this:

- Certain uncertainty
- Serious Playfulness
- Unquestioning questioning

The one thing we can be certain of in life is that very little is certain, and when we are using the reflective process in order to improve our practice this can be quite frustrating. In modern society we are used to having all the answers at our fingertips, so much so that a state of 'not knowing' can become very uncomfortable. Yet not knowing is probably the best educative state of mind, especially when the excitement of a new discovery begins to take hold. Schön (1983) referred to this as the 'swampy lowlands' to indicate situations of confusion where a usual technical solution is not readily available. In reflective practice this would mean encouraging uncertainty by thinking and acting as if you don't know and responding creatively to thoughts and events.

Serious playfulness simply means trying out new things. It is a way of making the process more dynamic in that we are playing with ideas and in doing so accepting that reflective practice can be a process of looking for something even when we are not sure what it is. Anything and everything can be questioned, enjoying a circuitous route rather than a direct journey from problem to solution. Dewey (1910) referred to playfulness as an attitude of mind, suggesting that the development of playfulness was a path to freedom: 'To be playful and serious at the same time is possible, and it defines the ideal mental condition' (Dewey, 1910: 218).

The third foundation, unquestioning questioning, is about accepting that the process will involve more questions than answers. Questions will prompt the paths we take and determine our findings. This strategy doesn't allow anything to be taken for granted and can be a creative release of everyday assumptions as well as the discovery of other possible ways of being. It is much like the Socratic approach (Socrates based his pedagogic method on questions) and has a focus on the journey of exploration.

> In a nutshell – this model has a focus on challenging accepted ideas and norms of practice. It is a creative approach which relies on making familiar things strange in order to explore them from a range of angles.

Socratic questioning

Whichever model of reflection we choose to adopt, the framework will be one which encourages us to question, and using a Socratic approach may be useful here. The Socratic method is based on six types of questions that question assumptions and help clarify thinking. The first category is conceptual clarification:

* What exactly does this mean?
* Give me an example of . . .
* Are you saying . . . or . . . ?

These questions prompt thinking about reasoning and making connections between concepts and real-life examples. They can be followed by probing your assumptions:

* How did you choose those assumptions?
* What else could we assume?
* How can you verify/disprove that assumption?

A similar type of question is one which probes rationale:

- How do you know this?
- What do you think causes . . . ?
- What evidence is there to support what you are saying? How might it be refuted?

Alternatively, we could question viewpoints or perceptions:

- What alternative ways are there of looking at this?
- What is the difference between . . . and . . . ?
- What would . . . say about it?

Probing implications and consequences takes this a step further and provides an opportunity to check if assumptions make sense:

- What are the implications of . . . ?
- How does . . . affect . . . ?
- How does . . . fit with what we learned before?

A final strategy is to ask questions about the question, for example:

- What was the point of asking that question?
- Why do you think I asked you this question?

Using a Socratic questioning approach is a constructive way of challenging thinking and offers a foundation for deeper reflection, which may in turn provide the fuel for interesting insights (Thompson, 2019).

The models of reflection outlined in this chapter have been selected because they provide different structures for what is essentially the same process, and as shown in Figure 2.1 there are a range of approaches you can take. Each offers something different and the decision about which model to adopt (or adapt) may simply be a matter of personal preference, but it is worth spending a few minutes thinking about how the models might work in practice. Consider the following scenarios; based on what you now know about models of reflection, which would you select?

Ameena was new to her role and keen to make an impression. She attended every team meeting and wanted to ensure that her presence was noted, something she did by ensuring she made a contribution to the meeting. At first this was acknowledged enthusiastically by other members of the team but more recently seemed to be less welcome. No-one had actually said anything about it, but she had noticed that others were no longer encouraging her to speak or acknowledging her comments when she did. She knew something had changed – she just didn't know what it was.

Mollie had been in her new job for two months and was beginning to feel the challenges of managing a dysfunctional team. They didn't seem to communicate and had taken to using her as a sounding board to complain about each other. Her own manager had warned her that this might be the problem and had outlined the various strategies that her predecessor had implemented in order to solve the problem, all of which had limited success. She knew what hadn't worked . . . now all she needed to do was to work out what might work.

Something had changed for Ameena – a strategy she had used previously was no longer working, so it seems she needs to work out two things. What had changed – was there something different about how she was contributing to meetings? Were others perceiving her contributions in a different way? The second thing she might want to think about is what she could do differently when she was next in a team meeting. If Ameena wants to view this from different perspectives, then using Brookfield's model might work well as this would provide a focus on others' views as well as reviewing potential alternatives via the theoretical lens. Also, Gibbs' model would help to establish an objective view of events and would prompt some ideas for potential changes.

In Mollie's case, she is armed with previous data in that her own manager has information regarding strategies that have already been tried. This is a useful starting point as Mollie already has some empirical knowledge as well as her own personal experiences of working with the team. Johns' model seems like a good fit here and would provide a useful framework for digging a little deeper into the issues. An alternative might be to sit with the discomfort of not resolving the issue straight away and take a 'through the looking glass' approach in order to generate some creative options.

In truth, any of the models could be applied in either of the situations – as could any other model taken from the examples in Figure 3.2. The purpose of this activity is to mentally work through the ideas to see which feels like a good fit for you.

Mental maps and theories in use

In chapter one we looked at the notion of *Weltanshauung* to provide an explanation of the natural tendency to interpret aspects of our lives in habitual ways. Mental maps are a similar concept and relate to an individual's internal understanding of their world and the subsequent impact this has on actions. Argyris and Schön (1974), inspired by the work of Jung, take this one step further and propose that our mental maps inform how we might plan, implement and review our actions. They use the term 'theories in use' to describe this process and suggest that our theories in use are not necessarily in alignment with the things we say we do – which they call 'espoused theories'. Furthermore, they state that few people are aware that their theories in use, which dictate how they might approach a given task or behave in a particular situation, are actually different to the ones they espouse! Most of us can cite examples of these discrepancies from both personal and professional perspectives. For example, a colleague talks about how 'risk taking' is the very best way to develop your skills but is often the person most likely to follow formal protocols. Your married friend says she is envious of your single status and tells you that if she were single, she would have a great life living on her own without the bother of a partner. Unfortunately, your friend's wish is granted. Shocked and in a panic, what do you think she does? I will leave you to fill in the blanks, but taking into account that we are naturally drawn to what is familiar, it is probably safe to guess that the subsequent actions will not match her espoused theories.

So, in summary:

- Espoused theory – the views and values individuals believe their behaviour is based on. These are the things we say we might do in a given situation and represent the ideas, actions and values we align ourselves with.
- Theory in use – the views and values implied by actions and behaviours.

The concept of espoused theories and theories in use is probably something most of us recognise in other people but neglect to see in ourselves! Argyris and Schön's work is based on a professional context although it was inspired by Jung's descriptions of the 'persona' (the image we present to others) as distinct from the 'shadow' which is made up of hidden anxieties and repressed thoughts (in Snowden, 2006). Jung maintained that any disunity between thoughts and conscious actions had the potential to generate internal conflicts and create anxieties and advocated bringing these thoughts into our conscious attention so that we might accommodate them. Similarly, disparities between theories in use and espoused theories may well highlight challenges to core values in relation to our professional role, and finding some alignment between the two may create potential for professional growth.

Johari's window

Johari's window (Luft & Ingham, 1955) is a well-known technique for improving self-knowledge through self-disclosure and feedback and provides an opportunity to uncover our espoused theories/theories in use as well as some aspects of what Jung described as 'shadow'. Figure 3.4

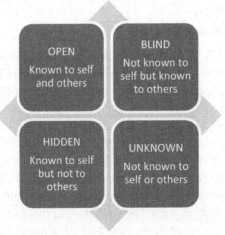

Figure 3.4 Johari's window

outlines the four quadrants of the model which represent aspects of self that we choose to share or not share with others:

Open – based on things in the public domain – the things you and others know about yourself, such as job role, specific skills and abilities that have already been demonstrated.

Blind – aspects of self that could be considered 'blind spots' – others may be aware of these things, but you are not. Typical examples would be displaying regular behaviours like interrupting others or not fully listening.

Hidden – represents things we know about ourselves, but we keep from others. These may be things we are not proud or ashamed of or things we feel others might disapprove of. It is quite natural for us to keep some information hidden, but there is also great potential in bringing some aspects into the open quadrant.

Unknown – may contain a variety of things such as latent aptitudes. This might include under-estimating skills, conditioned behaviours or beliefs developed in childhood. This area can be uncovered through creative reflection as well as feedback from others . . . sometimes by simply trying new things and reflecting on the experience.

10-Minute Reflection

Johari's window can be a powerful tool for examining aspects of ourselves we keep hidden or are not in our awareness. Ideally, the tool should be used with support from someone you trust to help you explore (such as a friend or mentor), but it can quite easily be done alone and then discussed at a later date. Using the example quadrant in Figure 3.4 as a guide, drawn up your own quadrant as honestly as you can. Then when you are ready, discuss this with someone else (or get someone to go through the process with you). Remember this is not about judgement, it is simply about bringing things into awareness so that they may be explored further.

Chapter reflections

In this chapter we have considered the importance of structuring reflection and have explored a number of reflective models to help with this. The models all have something to offer, and what and how they are used is very much personal choice. However, it is worth remembering that they are only models and as such have limitations. When reflecting on professional practice we are usually considering our own actions as well as interactions with others, and these are not always simple problem-to-solution scenarios. Therefore flexibility is paramount in order to provide a pathway for thoughts to evolve. Sometimes this means mean owning up to things we would rather keep under wraps, practising authenticity and at times making ourselves vulnerable. Some questions to consider as you move forwards are the ways in which reflection can help support your practice and the specific things you would like to get out of the process. It is also worth considering what potential barriers there are for you to reflect honestly on your thoughts and actions.

References

Argyris, M., & Schön, D. (1974) *Theory in Practice. Increasing Professional Effectiveness*. San Francisco, CA: Jossey-Bass.

Atkins, S., & Murphy, K. (1993) 'Reflection a Review of the Literature'. *Journal of Advanced Nursing*, 18(8): 1188-1192.

Bolton, G. (2001) *Reflective Practice: Writing and Professional Development*. London: Paul Chapman Publishing Ltd.

Bolton, G. (2010) *Reflective Practice, Writing and Professional Development*. London: Sage Publications.

Boud, D., Cohen, R., & Walker, D. (1985) *Reflection: Turning Experience into Learning*. London: Kogan Page.

Brookfield, S. (1998) 'Critically Reflective Practice'. *The Journal of Continuing Education in the Health Professions*, 18: 197-205.

Brookfield, S. (2017) *Becoming a Critically Reflective Teacher*. San Francisco, CA: John Wiley and Sons.

Carper, B. (1978) 'Fundamental Patterns of Knowing in Nursing'. *Advances in Nursing Science*, 1(1): 13-23.

Carroll, L. (1871) *Through the Looking Glass and What Alice Found There*. London: Palgrave Macmillan.

Dewey, J. (1910) *How We Think*. Boston, MA: D C Heath & Co.

Gibbs, G. (1998) *Learning by Doing: A Guide to Teaching and Learning Methods*. Oxford: Further Education Unit, Oxford Polytechnic.

Johns, C. (ed.) (2017) *Becoming a Reflective Practitioner* (5th ed.). Hoboken, NJ: Wiley & Sons Ltd.

Luft, J., & Ingham, H. (1955) 'The Johari Window, a Graphic Model of Interpersonal Awareness'. In *Proceedings of the Western Training Laboratory in Group Development*. Los Angeles, CA: University of California.

Mezirow, J. (1997) *Transformative Dimensions of Adult Learning*. San Francisco, CA: Jossey-Bass.

Milne, A. A. (1926) *Winnie the Pooh*. London: Methuen.

Schön, D. A. (1983) *The Reflective Practitioner: How Professionals Think in Action*. New York, NY: Basic Books.

Snowden, R. (2006) *Jung – The Key Ideas*. Oxon: Hodder Education.

Thompson, C. (2019) *The Magic of Mentoring – Developing Others and Yourself*. Oxon: Routledge.

Thompson, C., & Wolstencroft, P. (2018) 'No More Superheroes – Only Avatars – Survival Role Play in Post Compulsory Education'. In B. Merrill, A. Galimberti, A. Nizinska, & J. Gonzalez-Monteagudo (eds.), *Continuity and Discontinuity in Learning Careers: Potentials for a Learning Space in a Changing World*. Rotterdam: Sense.

Figure 4.1 Chapter mindmap

4 The importance of critical thinking

One of the dangers of developing the reflective habit is that it can so easily become a comfort blanket. The very process of writing down your thoughts is therapeutic and the temptation to make sense of events in ways which are acceptable to our sensitivities is a strong one. Of course, the opposite can also be true whereby reflections can become a form of unhelpful self-flagellation, but we will explore that idea in a later chapter. According to Dewey, 'thinking' represents a sort of back and forth volley between facts and understandings whereby fragmentary thoughts are adjusted by the addition of connecting links in order to find meaning: 'The meaning suggested supplies a mental platform, an intellectual point of view, from which to note and define the data more carefully' (1910: 79). The danger here is that meaning, once discovered, can be difficult to redefine, particularly if the processes of discovery was hard won. In this chapter we consider the importance of critical thinking and will discuss some strategies for improving criticality in our reflective practice.

The impact of our thoughts

There is a well-known quote from *Hamlet* which expresses the importance of thought succinctly: 'There is nothing either good or bad but thinking makes it so' (Shakespeare, Act 2 scene 2). This really sums up why reflection is such an important process as it offers the opportunity to filter the thousands of things going through our minds – a little like Dumbledore's 'Pensieve', an enchanted tool allowing the Wizard to revisit memories and thoughts. (Rowling, 2014).

Thinking about the way we think is certainly something that has changed over the last 40 or 50 years, but recognition of the impact of our thoughts has not. Shakespeare's Hamlet seems to have made a very pertinent point. Most of us are quite good at ruminating to the extent that we come to very firm conclusions about things – often judgements about ourselves. When we arrive at a particular conclusion, such as, 'I am not good at job interviews', the likelihood is that we will do two things to support this. The first is to discount anything that may contradict this belief and the second is to find evidence to reinforce it. This can turn into something of a vicious cycle as we are continually caught up in the process of proving our initial hypothesis!

In his work on learned helplessness, Seligman considers the impact of thoughts on feelings and behaviours and advocates that it is just as possible to learn optimism as it is to

DOI: 10.4324/9781003056812-5

learn helplessness. 'Habits of thinking need not be forever. One of the most significant find-ings in psychology in the last twenty years is that individuals can choose the way they think' (Seligman, 2018: 8). He suggests that the way we think and the way that we talk about our successes and failures has an impact on all aspects of our lives including achievement and health. Similarly, Dweck's findings in her work on mindset highlighted the impact of the way we think about our abilities on our overall achievements. Dweck believes that success has more to do with our approach to something than any innate talents we may have and advo-cates the development of a growth mindset which has a focus on finding strategies that help to achieve goals (Dweck, 2017). If we adopt a growth mindset we are less likely to dismiss something because we don't feel we have an innate talent for it and more likely to find strate-gies to help us learn the skills we need, thereby developing the belief that we have 'untapped' rather than 'fixed' potential.

The idea that changing the way you think can change your life outcomes is an attractive one – but is it simply a case of thinking positively and developing a growth mindset?

> Caitlin was determined to change her life. So far she had experienced a range of dull jobs and disappointing relationships. At 37 she knew it was about time to make some changes, so she enrolled herself in some workshops to begin her transformation. After attending 'Believe in yourself', 'Achieve your dreams' and 'Becoming successful in every aspect of life' she felt she was equipped with the tools to move forwards. She now knew that the key was to take a more positive approach and everything else would fall into place. Every morning she started the day with an affirmation and told herself that today would be a positive day. Every evening she practised gratitude and reviewed progress against her goals.
>
> After several weeks she was still in a dull job and no sign of Prince Charming – what was she doing wrong?

In theory, there is nothing wrong with Caitlin's approach. After all the initial burst of enthusi-asm was probably the result of attending motivating workshops, and personally I would pre-fer to attend something that gives me a motivation boost than something that sends me to sleep. However, it is important to understand the impact of this in the longer term: 'Seminars can hike motivation and leave employees pumped-up and exuberant. Yet these ardours are ephemeral. . . . Pumping up seminars work for a few days or weeks, then more pumping up is needed' (Seligman, 2018: 13). Learned optimism goes beyond positive thinking or the use of positive affirmations: 'We have found over the years that positive statements you make to yourself have little if any effect. What is crucial is what you think when you fail . . . changing the destructive things you say to yourself when you experience the setbacks that life deals all of us is the central skill of optimism' (Seligman, 2018: 15).

My personal belief is that in general taking a positive approach to life is more beneficial than not, but positive thinking applied as a panacea can actually lead to delusion and a false sense of growth. We do not develop simply by adopting a growth mindset or learning how to be more optimistic – we develop by increasing our awareness, by generating trust in our ability to make changes and in taking active steps to overcome challenges. In the example of Caitlin, she had benefited from the motivation burst accompanying the seminars but had omitted to consider the practical actions that could support her desired changes. As a result, she may be in danger of falling into a negative spiral because she has not achieved her goals. It is easier to say that something just didn't work and then give up than it is to challenge our approach. Just think about the millions made in the dieting industry based on the premise that people will try and fail but continue to hope that trying the next thing will work. At no point is there a realisation that the problem lies in habitual behaviours rather than a specific eating plan.

Our thinking has a significant impact on our behaviours, but it is the quality of our thinking, 'thinking well' that makes the real difference.

Thinking can be an automatic process representing everything that is 'in our heads' or 'goes through our minds' (Dewey, 1910: 2), but 'thinking well' may take a little more effort. Research has outlined two systems at play:

1   Automatic thinking is intuitive and fast. This is the type of thinking that requires minimal effort and often links to familiar things or things we may consider inconsequential. The many decisions we might make whilst driving a car or briefly noticing the way that someone responded to something we said.
2   Deliberate thinking is slow and conscious. This type of thinking requires focus and effort. We might use this when making decisions, when explaining something to someone else or when trying to resolve a problem (Kahneman, 2011).

The first type of thinking is essential in carrying out our day-to-day activities and is essential in juggling the many demands on our time. After all, who has time to contemplate every single thing they do? But it is also the type of thinking that will lead to automatic responses, which, it could be argued, may not be the product of thought at all! When we process thoughts very quickly we are also likely to get things wrong. Even when using the slow and deliberate approach it is possible to make errors, and we may need to include additional strategies to not only slow up the process of our thinking but to improve the quality of it.

When you consider some of the models of reflection outlined in Chapter 3, it is easy to get the impression that when reflecting we need to organise our thoughts immediately so that we not only have a deeper understanding of an issue but that we can also come up with an active strategy to apply to it. That may happen at times, but often it is necessary to slow down deliberate thinking even further in order to avoid jumping to the wrong conclusions or coming up with quick-fix strategies that simply put a plaster on the wound. *Incubation* is a term used in psychology to describe an aspect of thinking often associated with creativity. It is a process of recombining elements of thought in ways that were initially hidden. To create a period of incubation is to consciously stop thinking about something and to do something else until at a later point the solution 'magically' appears. The thought or problem is put to one side, during which time some unconscious processing occurs that provides further insight (Ohlsson, 1992; Wallas, 1926).

5-Minute Reflection Strategy: Doodling

Take your focus away from your conscious thoughts by spending five minutes doodling or colouring something in. Choose something that doesn't require you to think too much, simply get engrossed in the activity.

The doodling strategy is a way of creating an incubation period. Five minutes is unlikely to be enough, but it is a start and this is something you can go back to whenever you need to be distracted. Doing something at a level of unconscious competence means that you are occupying your conscious brain with the task in hand and letting unconscious processing search for insight.

The thoughts and feelings connection

A key premise of Cognitive Behavioural Therapy (CBT) is that the messages we give ourselves have a significant impact on our emotions, which in turn will influence our actions and further thoughts. Butler *et al.* (2018) suggest that we might also think in images and don't necessarily cognize in words, so if we have had an interaction that has caused concern such as a time when we know we hurt someone, an image of that might come to mind rather than a description. In either case the thoughts and images will have an impact on how we feel and how we might follow up these feelings with actions. Therefore, the suggestion is that if we want to change negative feelings and achieve more positive outcomes, we need to change our thinking. A useful strategy is to outline types of 'twisted or distorted thinking and consider some alternative ways of framing the thoughts (Burns, 1990; Butler *et al.*, 2018). Some examples of these have been outlined in Table 4.1.

Table 4.1 Types of distorted thinking

Distorted Thinking	Examples
Generalisation – assuming that because something happened once, the same things will always happen. Often prefaced with words like 'always' or 'never'.	'I always get things wrong.' 'I never seem to say the right thing.' 'I am never the lucky one.'
All-or-nothing – things are seen as absolutes and there is a tendency to think in extremes without seeing a middle ground.	'If I can't do this perfectly – why bother?' 'That one mistake has ruined the whole thing.' 'One false move will blow the whole thing.'
Mind reading – based on the premise that we know what someone else is thinking even though we have no evidence.	'I know you don't believe me.' 'I know you are upset about that.' 'They think I am incompetent.'
Fortune telling – a form of distortion that often predicts a negative outcome without considering objective facts.	'I am not going to get that job.' 'This is bound to go wrong.' 'He/she hasn't been in touch yet, so I will never see them again.'

Distorted Thinking	Examples
Discounting positives - this is a negative filter whereby we may reject our efforts or skills as if they don't count. It can be seen as false modesty by some so has a double negative.	'He only said that to make me feel better.' 'I was just lucky.' 'I happened to be in the right place at the right time.'
Catastrophising - we predict the worst outcome and if something goes wrong it will be a 'disaster' or a 'nightmare'.	'If I make a mistake I will lose my job.' 'If this ends I will never be happy again.' 'If that happens I will lose my mind.'
Exaggerating - we do this when we give negative events more importance than they deserve and positive ones less importance.	'I can't bear this feeling.' 'People never enjoy being with me because ...' 'Being given that award doesn't really mean anything.'
Should and Must - these are generalisations that imply a rule and usually refer to beliefs about things we should, should not, must or must not do.	'I must not make mistakes.' 'I should be perfect.' 'We must follow the rules.'
Personalising - this happens when we take a very ego-based approach to events and see everything as being personal rather than evaluating the bigger picture.	'They didn't ask me because they don't like me.' 'They are ignoring me.' 'He failed because I didn't support him enough.'
Cause and effect - these thoughts are based on the idea that we are not in control of our emotional state and that one action will cause another reaction. This means that other people have control over how we feel.	'You make me angry.' 'The things you're saying are making me anxious.' 'You are making me nervous.'

Using Table 4.1 as a guide try to come up with some alternative statements to replace the examples of distorted thinking. For example, 'I am never the lucky one.' Could be replaced with, 'I seem to be experiencing some bad luck at the moment.' Or 'If I can't do this perfectly, why bother?' could become 'I may not do this perfectly, but I am going to put in my best effort.' Remember the statements need to be close to the original if they are to have impact – you may be tempted to change 'I am never the lucky one' to 'I am always the lucky one.' But that is an entirely different meaning and not representative of the original feeling.

Critical thinking

It is important to draw the distinction between critical thinking and criticism as this is often a point of confusion. When we disagree with something we may be inclined to criticise by highlighting a fault. For example 'I feel that Thompson's description of critical thinking is flawed.' So far, so good. This statement certainly evidences a criticism and shows that the author doesn't necessarily agree with everything they read, but is it evidence of critical thinking? It actually evidences a judgement without a justification. In general, criticism is about finding fault with something, it is often aimed at a person rather than an argument and sometimes it is influenced by emotion. In the example, the author shows that they don't agree with something, but they are not providing any evidence of a reasoned argument – who is to say what specifically they don't like? Critical thinking outlines underlying assumptions in a piece of work and involves judgement. In addition, that judgement is justified with some evidence. In this case the author might have said, 'Thompson's description of critical thinking is flawed in one key respect: it does not take into account . . .' In this example the statement is more specific as it provides details of and aspect the author doesn't agree with or wants to challenge.

Brookfield (2012) suggests that there are four aspects of critical thinking:

- Hunting assumptions
- Checking assumptions
- Seeing things from different viewpoints
- Taking action

Our habits of thinking and most of our actions are based on assumptions that we have accepted as being accurate and these are often so embedded we are not even aware of their presence. Assumptions relate to the beliefs we have absorbed about our place in the world that give meaning to what we do and who we are. They often seem so obvious that they don't require further thought and may even be things we resist thinking about. Hunting assumptions is about uncovering some of these things in order to bring them into awareness. Brookfield outlines three different types of assumption: paradigmatic, prescriptive and causal:

Paradigmatic assumptions could be described as internalised beliefs. They are what we *know* to be true. They help us to structure our understanding of the world and our purpose within it. We may have a paradigmatic assumption that education is a social and democratic process which could be challenged when we consider the high cost of university fees.

Prescriptive assumptions relate to what we think should be happening in a particular situation. This could include the way someone should behave or things they should do. A prescriptive assumption might be that university students are autonomous learners and should take control of their own learning or that adults are sufficiently informed about healthy lifestyles and should take steps to look after body and mind.

Causal assumptions are about how different parts of the world interact and are based on a cause-and-effect relationship . . . if I do 'a' then 'b' will happen. A common assumption in teaching and learning is that it must be an active, rather than passive process. There is certainly some logic in that, but when you observe a lesson where the teacher has launched activity after activity, ensuring that learners were active throughout but where there was little evidence of sharing background knowledge or challenging misconceptions, this assumption might be challenged.

Raising awareness of assumptions is only the first step. Once assumptions have been highlighted it is important to check their validity. Checking assumptions can be done effectively by following a step-by-step process.

10-Minute Reflection Down the Rabbit Hole

1   Write down your assumptions (no editing).
2   Ask why – what is the reason for the assumption?
3   Examine the words . . . what are the meanings behind the words? Could these be redefined?
4   Hypothesise – imagine an assumption is removed. What would happen? What if you changed an aspect of it or replaced it with a different assumption?
5   Follow your thoughts down the rabbit hole by repeating each step to uncover further assumptions.

The down the rabbit hole technique is a strategy for analysing assumptions. It works best as an iterative process and the steps can be repeated with different assumptions.

Another strategy for testing out assumptions is to view them from different perspectives. In many of the roles each of us plays in life we may adopt a particular persona for example as teacher, parent, friend and in each case may well play a different role. Whilst in role our assumptions will be linked to whatever our key focus is, often forgetting that others within this scene may have an entirely different perspective. In Chapter 3 we discussed the four lenses model (Brookfield, 2017), which does just this by looking at a particular event from a personal viewpoint, then from the views of students, colleagues and theories.

Critical thinking

Critical thinking is something we all have the ability to do and probably something we all think we do reasonably well, particularly if we are reflective by nature. However, one important thing to remember is that there is also a social and emotional process at play. When we develop our ideas and learn new things we often do so in a social context and are influenced by those in close contact such as peers, teachers, friends and family. Learning, particularly the type of learning that is situated within day-to-day life, is often built up from a series of experiences and influences, and some of the things we learn, more specifically, the things we learn about ourselves, can be closely linked to emotions. Some things are easy to learn, others are not and of course the opposite is true . . . the process of thinking critically often means that there is a certain amount of unlearning that has to happen.

In Chapter 1 we briefly discussed Mezirow's ideas about disorientating dilemmas describing how unexpected situations challenge previous learning and provide the opportunity to transform our understandings. Research on transformative learning suggests that disorientating dilemmas create an awareness of conflicting thoughts and feelings and can lead to a reappraisal of our perspectives by offering opportunities to transform fixed assumptions and expectations. (Mezirow & Taylor, 2009). A disorientating dilemma is often a catalyst which doesn't fit with our expectations, something that actually forces a rethink, and it can often be the result of an event that is disruptive on a number of levels. For example, we may lose our job or our partner may decide to leave. Both have a significant impact on day-to-day life and force us to challenge our assumptions about our professional role and our relationships. Disorientating dilemmas can challenge us at a visceral level because they have the potential to shake up significant part of our lives, challenging things we thought we really understood. Changing those beliefs can be an uncomfortable process: 'The whole idea of systematically searching out assumptions is often deliberately avoided for fear of where it might lead. No one likes to discover that ideas they have lived by for much of their life are distorted and invalid' (Mezirow & Taylor, 2009: 57). Imagine the impact any of the following would have on you:

1   You have been working on an important project with a colleague you like and respect. You then discover they have been giving everyone the impression that they took charge of the project and that you did very little towards it.
2   Your boss is someone you really like and trust, but you have recently been presented with information that suggests they have abused their position of power for personal gain.
3   Last week, your partner of ten years told you how happy they were in your relationship. This week they tell you they have met someone else and want to leave.

All of these scenarios have the potential to encourage a questioning of values, judgements and perceptions. They may form the basis of genuine critical reflection in which we aim to objectively analyse the situation in order to learn from it. However, when we think we have a good understanding of something, to have that understanding challenged in such a stark way is not only disorientating but threatens to dismantle all previous beliefs and create cognitive dissonance. This produces a feeling of extreme discomfort that we need to address if we want to restore a sense of balance. According to Festinger (1957) we have an inner drive to hold all our attitudes and beliefs in harmony and avoid disharmony (dissonance), and we may need to change our beliefs about something in order to do this so potentially we could:

- Change our attitudes and/or beliefs;
- Acquire new information that helps reduce the dissonance;
- Use internal reasoning and justification to accommodate the dissonance.

In the examples provided the first might make us question our judgement about people – in order to restore some balance we might tell ourselves that the deceit wasn't intended or that we were overreacting. In example two we are faced with questioning our own values about integrity. We like and trust someone who has challenged that view – do we change how we feel about them or do we alter our perspective about what integrity means to us? Situation 3 is likely to challenge our understanding of personal relationships. In order to restore balance, we could tell ourselves that fidelity is not a fundamental component of a relationship or we might assign blame to a third party – both options provide the opportunity to make sense of the situation.

   In each of the three examples it is possible to challenge previously held values and beliefs, to develop new understandings and alter our frame of reference. It is also just as easy to find a justification for each of the scenarios which allows us to gloss over the event, to make an uncomfortable situation more comfortable; but if we really want to learn from the experience, is that the best approach? The way that we think about the situation will inform our actions, and it is only by critically examining events that we may also develop our understandings and take informed action.

Six strategies for critical thinking

The following strategies provide some simple techniques to help sharpen your critical thinking skills:

- *Flipping the questions* – This is a simple strategy based on questioning assumptions. The starting point is to consider some simple questions:
  - What information do I have about the situation?
  - What might I be overlooking?
  - What do I believe to be true?
  - What else could be true?

Then try to think in reverse by flipping the questions:

  - What information is missing?
  - What things do I need to know?
  - What do I believe to be false?
  - What else could be false?

This may seem counter-intuitive at first as you are likely to feel that you can't possibly know what information is missing, but it does jolt you out of thinking about the dilemma in the same way and that may provide new insights.

Assumptions inventory – this is simply a record of the key assumptions you are making about a given situation. When explaining something or reflecting on a specific point consider what the underlying assumptions are. This could be done simply by asking 'what assumptions am I making here?', which can then be challenged with 'what else could I assume?'

Speaking in tongues – this strategy is about viewing things from a range of perspectives and is designed to show how the same idea can be interpreted in different ways (Brookfield, 2012). In the example provided by Brookfield the technique is employed in teaching by posting signs around the classroom, each of which corresponds to a different school of thought on a topic. Then an overview is provided, and the presenter moves to each of the signs to present the topic from each of the viewpoints. This is extended by asking for questions and then moving to each of the signs and answering in a way that matches that school of thought.

Thinking hats – Although not specifically about criticality, this strategy encourages lateral thinking which will extend perspectives. The technique was devised by De Bono (2000) and is often used to generate solutions to problems by encouraging the exploration of a problem through a range of perspectives and forcing us to move away from our current viewpoint. The 'hats' each have a different colour and purpose as follows:

- White hat – considers the facts of the situation
- Yellow hat – focuses on the positives

- Black hat – represents judgement and focusses on dangers and difficulties
- Red hat – signifies feelings – when 'wearing' this hat you are encouraged to express things such as likes and dislikes
- Green hat – has a focus on creativity, seeking out new ideas or possibilities
- Blue hat – manages the overall process – it keeps the others under control and ensures that guidelines are followed

Summary Rewrite – Write an account of whatever you want to reflect on, a situation you have encountered, a dilemma or something that has made you question your views on something. Go back and highlight the key points or phrases. Then restate these using different words. According to Newberg & Waldman (2012) words have a potent connection to emotions and the words we use have the potential to hurt or heal. When we first write our account, it may well be peppered with the emotion attached to whatever we are describing, but when we choose different words it is possible to introduce a higher degree of objectivity.

Storyboard – This is an effective strategy for those who prefer to think in images. Using a sheet of A4 paper landscape, set out a number of boxes as if you were preparing a comic strip. Populate these with images which tell the story of whatever you are reflecting on. You are limited to the space on the page, which means that you have to extract the key points and are forced to make decisions about what is important.

Chapter reflections

In this chapter we have considered the impact of thought on developing understandings and generating behaviours. In addition, the focus on critical thinking as a vehicle for locating and analysing assumptions which in turn influence beliefs and actions has provided the scope to consider some practical strategies that might be employed. In all of this it is important to acknowledge that habits apply to thinking as much as they do to day-to-day routines, and it is only in taking time to recognise and address these habits that we are providing the space to think more critically.

References

Brookfield, S. (2012) *Teaching for Critical Thinking – Tools and Techniques to Help Students Question Their Assumptions*. San Francisco, CA: John Wiley and Sons.

Brookfield, S. (2017) *Becoming a Critically Reflective Teacher*. San Francisco, CA: John Wiley and Sons.

Burns, D. D. (1990) *The Feeling Good Handbook*. Middlesex: Penguin.

Butler, G., Grey, N., & Hope, T. (2018) *Managing Your Mind – The Mental Fitness Guide* (3rd ed.). Oxford: Oxford University Press.

De Bono, E. (2000) *Six Thinking Hats*. London: Penguin.

Dewey, J. (1910) *How We Think*. Boston, MA: Boston, MA: D C Heath & Co.

Dweck, C. (2017) *Mindset – Changing the Way You Think to Fulfil Your Potential*. London: Constable and Robinson Ltd.

Festinger, L. (1957) *A Theory of Cognitive Dissonance*. Stanford, CA: Stanford University Press.

Kahneman, D. (2011) *Thinking, Fast and Slow*. London: Penguin.

Mezirow, J., & Taylor, E. (2009) *Transformative Learning in Practice: Insights from Community, Workplace, and Higher Education*. San Francisco, CA: Jossey-Bass.

Newberg, A., & Waldman, M. R. (2012) *Words Can Change Your Brain*. New York, NY: Plume.

Ohlsson, S. (1992) 'Information Processing Explanations of Insight and Related Phenomena'. In M. T. Keane & K. J. Gilhooly (eds.), *Advances in the Psychology of Thinking*. London: Harvester Wheatsheaf.

Rowling, J. K. (2014) *Harry Potter and the Goblet of Fire*. New York, NY: Bloomsbury Children's Books.

Seligman, M (2018) *Learned Optimism: How to Change Your Mind and Your Life*. London: Nicholas Brealey Publishing.

Shakespeare, W. (2016) *Hamlet, Prince of Denmark* (C. Watts & K. Carabine, eds.). Herts: Wordsworth Editions. (Original work published 1599).

Wallas, G. (1926) *The Art of Thought*. London: Cape.

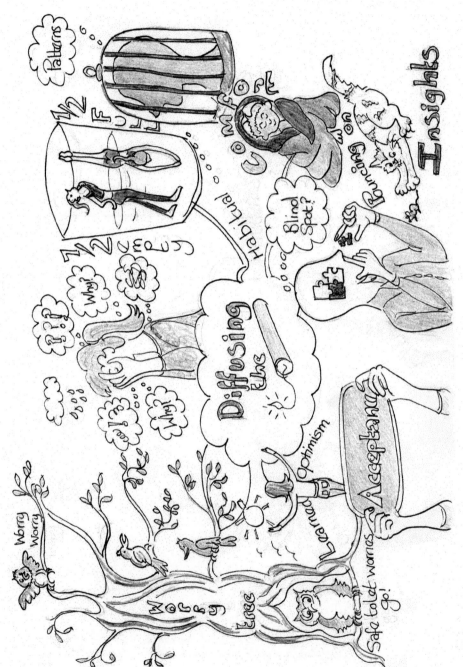

Figure 5.1 Chapter mindmap

5 Defusing the dynamite

In the previous chapter we discussed the ways in which reflection can develop into a type of 'comfort blanket', keeping us cosily ensconced in ways of thinking which reinforce current perceptions. We also considered some aspects of distorted thinking which can lead to unhelpful beliefs and potentially vicious cycles. If done well, reflective practice can be one of the most effective tools for improving not only what we do but how we choose to be. However, it can also have a dark side. The process of reflection has an emotional element and can be harmful when it turns into negative rumination or self-flagellation. As Brookfield says '[it] is like laying down charges of psychological dynamite. When these assumptions explode . . . the whole structure of our assumptive world crumbles' (Brookfield, 1990: 178). In this chapter we will explore some of these ideas and consider strategies for reframing unhelpful reflections.

Reflection and introspection

When we reflect, we are usually considering a particular event from a range of perspectives in order to establish as objective an account as possible. Introspection is more personal as its focus is on looking inwards by analysing our own thoughts and feelings. We do this in reflection too, so the boundaries are blurred – the key difference is the focus. Introspection could be described as a more ego-centric form of reflection which has as its main aim the development of self-awareness. It can provide a useful source of personal knowledge which helps us to make connections between a range of experiences as well as providing the forum from which to analyse our responses to them. Introspection which leads to greater self-awareness is also something which will help increase emotional intelligence which, according to Goleman, enhances our chances of career success (Goleman, 1996). All well and good, but is it possible to have too much introspection?

One thing we should consider is that the very act of analysing our thoughts and feelings in some way changes them. Through the process we learn to think about things in different ways and in an ideal world these different perceptions will challenge habitual patterns and extend our awareness. However, this isn't always the case and one danger to be aware of is confirmation bias. This represents a tendency to interpret things in ways which confirm already held beliefs. It is a sort of cognitive bias that can distort events by the way that we think about them. You might notice this in others when they appear to have selective

DOI: 10.4324/9781003056812-6

memories or when they are reflecting and focus on aspects of a situation that they consider important – often being drawn to things that support existing understandings.

Having a greater understanding of ourselves is helpful and is believed to support our relationships, well-being and happiness. It is also suggested that people with high insight generally feel more in control of life and have more personal growth (Harrington & Loffredo, 2010). However, some studies state that there is actually no relationship between introspection and insight (Grant *et al.*, 2002). The act of thinking about ourselves isn't necessarily the same as knowing ourselves, suggesting that we can potentially spend hours in the process of introspection and have no more insight that when we started!

It is also possible for introspection to cloud our self-perception, particularly if we are desperately searching for answers. Sometimes it can result in a vicious cycle of negative thinking,. For examples of this, go back to the types of distorted thinking outlined in Chapter 4.

Zoe was hoping to gain a promotion to a more senior role, and luckily an opportunity she could apply for had just come up. Zoe was offered an interview and although she suspected she was only invited because she already worked in the relevant team, she was pleased. That was until she started to prepare for the event. For days she agonized over the questions she might be asked and the fact that she *always* got tongue-tied when she was nervous, and she *knew* she would be nervous. Also, she *knew* that the manager leading the interviews didn't think she was experienced enough for the job, so she probably didn't have a chance of getting it anyway. Actually she wasn't at all sure why she was putting herself through this at all, may as well just back out. When the interview came around, Zoe tried to put on her best face. She was honest and open with the panel and decided to address any concerns from the outset – so, she started by letting them know that she understood that they thought she didn't have enough experience and continued to tell them all the negative 'truths' that she had been ruminating on over in the last few days.

The type of introspection which leads to rumination can cloud our perceptions and lead to unintended consequences. In Zoe's case this probably led to not being offered a job she wanted and was probably very capable of doing. If you look back at the examples of distorted thinking in Chapter 4 – how many of them do you see here? There is certainly evidence of mind reading – Zoe 'knew' the manager leading the interviews didn't think she was experienced enough. There was a certain amount of fortune telling as she was already convinced she didn't have a chance of getting the job and of course the generalisation about always getting tongue-tied. All of that added to what for many people is a stressful situation anyway.

But don't put this book down just yet! I do realise that many of the things I have said in this chapter may appear contradictory to the comments made in previous chapters. This isn't intended to add confusion but to offer a more balanced perspective – whilst I do think reflection is a highly effective strategy for personal and professional development, I am also aware that it isn't a fool-proof process, and it is very important to be aware of potential barriers.

Reflection and indeed introspection can still be effective if space is created for developing awareness – this means being aware of confirmation bias. It is also important to be open to new ideas before leaping to judgements based on habitual ways of thinking. The final and probably most important point is that reflection should be a vehicle for developing curiosity, which in turn will open up new avenues and enhance flexibility. Reflection should be an adventure traversing new landscapes, not the trudging of a well-worn path to the same destination. Reflection and introspection both have a part to play in this adventure; we just need to be wary of the potential pitfalls – including our own eagerness to find answers. Pouncing on 'insights' is not always a solution. Sometimes we need to think critically in order to test out their validity and subsequent value.

5-Minute Reflection Strategy: What not Why?

When we examine thoughts and feelings or consider the way we behaved in a particular situation we often do this from the perspective of why? Why did I say that thing? Why did I do that? Why am I feeling this way? In doing this we will be seeking believable answers – and often what makes them believable is that they confirm what we already 'know'. In your next reflection try switching the why questions for what questions. For example, 'What did I say?', 'What was I feeling?', even 'What was good about that?', 'What could have been better?'

According to Eurich (2018) 'why?' is not an effective question for raising self-awareness as we don't have access to all of the unconscious thoughts and feelings that inform our actions and, as a result, tend to create answers that might feel true for us (but can be wrong). As our judgements are usually biased, it is likely that asking why leads to answers which confirm this bias. In contrast, asking 'what?' allows us to stay objective as we are not forcing judgements in order to answer the questions. Asking someone why they are feeling down about something will probably receive an answer confirming previously held beliefs, whereas asking 'What situations are you feeling down about?' requires more specific thought and may lead to uncovering blind spots that are potential areas for action. Blind spots, which refer to the things we may not be aware of but others can often see, are obviously difficult to highlight without some form of collaboration to help seek them out. In Chapter 3 we discussed Johari's window (Luft & Ingham, 1955) as a potential strategy for raising awareness of blind spots but there are other strategies which could be employed, such as peer mentoring, or, for a more formal approach, 360-degree appraisals where feedback from a range of people is sought. One thing to remember is that we have blind spots for a reason, and they are usually present because of some aspects of ourselves that we don't want to accept because it doesn't fit in with our overall values or worldview.

Acceptance

Increasingly we are surrounded by images of 'perfection', beautiful Instagram photographs, or Facebook posts depicting someone's 'so-much-better-than-ours' life that it takes a very self-assured person not to feel a sense of failure at times. It is also easy to see why there are some aspects of our self that we don't readily accept and that we might want to hide from others – after all, if social media is to be believed, everyone else is not only perfect, they have perfect lives! However, the practice of acceptance is a first step towards transformation as it not only enhances self-understanding but begins the process of removing barriers to change. Rogers understood this perfectly: 'I find I am more effective when I can listen acceptantly to myself, and can be myself. . . . the curious paradox is that when I accept myself just as I am, then I change' (Rogers, 1961: 17).

Although it is natural to do so, when we avoid aspects of ourselves that we don't like we also limit self-awareness, and it is the practice of acceptance that helps us to alter attitudes by slowly moving to kindness rather than judgement. This creates the foundation to under-standing the present and accepting where we are now so that we can step from the past into the future (Butler *et al.*, 2018).

Most people probably have aspects of their life that they would prefer to forget or not even acknowledge and integrating these is a process. The change curve (Kubler-Ross, 2005) illustrates this by showing the phases someone goes through when experiencing significant change. This was originally developed to try to gain a deeper understanding of dealing with grief, but it is also a useful model for understanding how we accept change.

In the denial stage there is shock and disbelief that the change is really happening and typical behaviours at this stage are to go on as if nothing has happened. Someone might

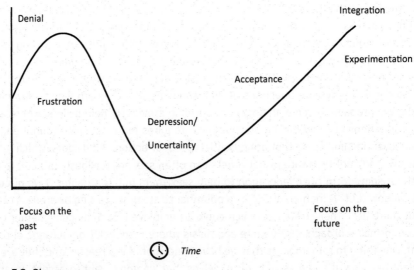

Figure 5.2 Change curve
Source: Adapted from Kubler-Ross (2005)

continue to do their job in the same way despite a demotion or make meals for a loved one whose departure is imminent. This 'business as usual' approach is a form of dissent against something we have not yet accepted. Frustration follows when we fully recognise that something is significantly different – the realisation of the event has hit and likely reactions include anger at self and others. Depression and uncertainty is depicted at the lowest point of the curve and this stage will include sadness, regret and fear for the future.

When the realisation that denial is futile finally strikes, the process of acceptance begins. At this stage there is a sense of resignation to the situation which leads the way to acceptance. Although this isn't necessarily a 'happy place', it is a significant step to moving on. Experimentation follows as acceptance grows and at this point the inevitably of change meets with a willingness to explore options. Finally, the stage of integration is the point at which the change becomes the new normal.

Acceptance is the foundation for change that leads to full integration of new events. It is being mindful of where we are at this point which is a first step to removing any obstacles to moving on. Acceptance is an attitude we are choosing whilst acknowledging that the change itself is not something we have control over, but our response to it is entirely in our choice. Victor Frankl makes this very clear when he writes about his harrowing experiences in the concentration camps during World War II: 'When we are no longer able to change a situation – we are challenged to change ourselves' (Frankl, 2004: 116).

Managing vulnerability

In this world of superficial perfection, embracing our own imperfections can be tricky – acknowledging failure may also mean acknowledging shame and being open to vulnerability. When you live in a society built on stories of success, owning your least successful moments is a challenge, but according to Brown (2012) this is about practising authenticity as well as opening up to vulnerability. Brown defines vulnerability as: 'not winning or losing; it's having the courage to show up and be seen when we have no control over the outcome' (Ibid. 4). She also emphasizes the importance of taking ownership of our stories so that we are open to living a more wholehearted life. Like Rogers, Brown acknowledges the importance of acceptance in order to embrace change: 'The irony is that we attempt to disown our difficult stories to appear more whole or more acceptable, but our wholeness – even our wholeheartedness – actually depends on the integration of our experiences, including the falls' (Brown, 2015: 43).

> Outwardly, Stefan's life was a success. He was well liked and respected in his career, had a stable relationship and a close group of friends. Very often he was the 'go to guy' when someone else wanted support because of his calming presence – a status he very much wanted to maintain. He worked hard at his career and also at supporting those around him. His life was full and days seemed to fly by. Most of the time he felt he was doing OK. His life was steady, an even keel; he wasn't riding the waves but was chugging along without any drama and although he often felt very tired by the endless round of work and home duties, this was the way he liked things.

As his next holiday approached, Stefan started to feel a little anxious. He had no difficulty with day-to-day life, but when every hour wasn't filled with activity his mind began to wander and he would find himself ruminating on past events. Sometimes his thoughts started off positively, when he remembered moments of joy or inspiration, but they always degenerated into a vicious spiral and became dominated by feelings of shame that he wasn't 'good enough'. At these points he would start to feel overwhelmed by his 'failures' and would end a period of rumination by resolving to do better – which usually meant filling his days with even more of what currently occupied them.

Stefan's story is one of someone who seems to hide from vulnerability by filling life with activity. In a sense, this might seem like a very healthy attitude in that it is a strategy for avoiding negative rumination, but it could also be viewed as avoidance. Covering the things we don't like with an ever-increasing range of activity will not only lead to exhaustion, it is also very effective smokescreen for blind spots and may deter the positive action required for a more authentic approach. As mentioned earlier in the chapter, blind spots are there for a reason and normally cover some aspect of ourselves that doesn't fit with the image we choose to present to the world. They can be difficult to uncover but may also be a really valuable point of reflection. The 'Feared Fantasy' technique (Burns, 2020) is a strategy that can be used to help discover as well as confront them. It is something you could use in a role play scenario if you want to work with someone else or as a written reflection. Burns describes this as entering 'An *Alice in Wonderland* nightmare world where there are two really weird rules. First, people really *are* having negative thoughts about you. Second, they aren't polite but get right up in your face and tell you what they think . . . In addition, they aren't nice about it . . . and try to put you down and humiliate you' (page 243). This sounds like quite an extreme strategy but it is based on the premise that when you face your fears you realise that 'the monster has no teeth' (Ibid.).

10-Minute Reflection Strategy – Feared Fantasy

Step one – write down all the negative thoughts you think others might be having about you. The sort of things that people might ordinarily think but wouldn't say. From a professional perspective mine might include: 'She is difficult to work with', 'She can be very disorganised.' Some scary personal ones might include: 'She can be boring' or 'She is not good enough.' Be honest – what are your most feared judgements?

Step two – write out a dialogue between a critic and yourself. The aim is for the critic to highlight your feared judgements in a very direct way and for you to respond with a combination of self-defence and acceptance. In self-defence you will let your critic know that what they are saying isn't true. Then using acceptance, you will agree with the critic with a sense of humour and inner peace. For example:

Critic: You can be really difficult to work with. Why do you always have to disagree with things?

You: That may be true, but the way I see it, I am bringing a different perspective.

Critic: That's what you call it! Honestly, it's a wonder you still have a job. Why can't you just shut up and get on with it?

You: I imagine a lot of my colleagues want to say that to me ☺ . . . but I care about what I do and I think it is important that as a team we consider a range of options. Overall, this has to improve our decision-making.

This technique is really a way of dealing with the projection of your own self-critical thoughts, as Burns says: 'You're really doing battle with yourself' (Ibid. 245). The aim is that by accepting the self-criticism and not feeling the need to defend it, the 'monster' is less powerful . . . your acceptance has helped to remove its teeth!

Learned optimism

Categorizing people into the grouping of optimist or pessimist is common practice. These are familiar terms and form a part of everyday language. We generally recognise optimistic or pessimistic tendencies in others by the way they talk about things and by their general approach to life. It is often referred to as 'Glass half empty' - the pessimistic approach which focusses on what is missing, or 'Glass half full' -the opposite focus. To those people with an optimistic outlook, pessimists might seem to have a downer on everything, always keen to find the negative in any situation, whereas those with a more pessimistic outlook, might describe optimists as being unrealistic, even delusional. Most of us can probably cite examples which fit both of these descriptions - but why is this important? Are we simply an optimist or pessimist and that's that? And if we are does it matter?

Seligman (2006), a researcher whose original focus was on helplessness, outlines the impact of thoughts on actions: 'Our thoughts are not merely reactions to events; they change what ensues' (page 5). After recognising that some subjects in his studies did not actually respond to stressful situations by showing signs of helplessness, he began to think about what it was that made some people give up when they face difficulties whilst others continue on. He used the term 'explanatory style' to explain this: 'Your habitual way of explaining bad events, your explanatory style, is more than just the words you mouth when you fail. It is a habit of thought, learned in childhood and adolescence . . . it is the hallmark of whether you are an optimist or a pessimist' (Ibid. 44).

Explanatory style is based on three key elements:

- Permanence
- Pervasiveness
- Personalisation

People who have a tendency to give up easily tend to explain bad events as if they are permanent - the bad events are something that will persist For example, 'I never get good

Figure 5.3 Glass half full

grades' as opposed to 'I didn't get a good grade in that test.' When bad things are considered permanent, this is viewed as a pessimistic explanatory style, whereas people who saw things as being less permanent, such as 'I didn't get a good grade in that test', are considered to have an optimistic explanatory style. However, when it comes to events perceived as good, this is switched around For example, someone with a pessimistic style might dismiss a lucky event as a one-off – 'It was a stroke of luck' – and someone with an optimistic style might see these things as more permanent – 'I am lucky.'

Pervasiveness is used to describe whether or not an event is attributed to something specific or whether it is considered universal: 'Some people can put their troubles neatly into a box and go about their lives even when one important aspect of it – their job, for example, or their love life – is suffering. Others bleed all over everything' (Seligman, 2006: 46). This is similar to the form of distorted thinking called catastrophising (outlined in Chapter 4) and refers to making universal explanations for failure which suggest it would be easier just to give up. An optimistic explanatory style would make a very specific explanation – not all-pervasive. For example, someone who has had a few bad dates might say: 'I'm not attractive' – a somewhat pessimistic approach suggesting that there is no point in dating any more. Alternatively 'I'm not attractive to her' is likely to have a very different impact on feelings and a very different outcome in terms of whether the person continues to date or not.

A final aspect of explanatory style is personalisation – whether or not we blame ourselves or circumstances when things go wrong. People who blame themselves when something bad has happened may have low self-esteem as a consequence – the 'thing' happened because there is something wrong with them or they are 'no good'. In contrast, people who blame external events do not experience such a negative impact on their self-esteem – they have externalized the event and don't see their actions as having anything to do with it.

Seligman suggests that learning the skills of optimism will effect a change in explanatory style which in turn influences the choices we make and the actions we take. This is a very powerful claim. Indeed it is difficult to argue against it given the benefits to be derived from a more positive approach, but it should perhaps come with a caveat. Learned optimism is not a form of magical thinking. We still need to take responsibility and sometimes things are down to us and not the fault of external factors. 'Life inflicts the same setbacks and tragedies on the optimist as on the pessimist, but the optimist weathers them better . . . bounces back from defeat, and, with his life somewhat poorer, he picks up and starts again' (Ibid. 207).

Strategies for reframing negative thoughts

As outlined in Chapter 1, we interact with the world based on our mental representations of it and of course sometimes, these representations are not accurate. Our emotions and behaviours are not necessarily determined by life events but by our perception of events – this has been a theme running throughout the book which emphasises the intense connection between thoughts and feelings. However, we don't always consider the consequences of this. When assumptions are irrational, they may cause inappropriate behaviours and will in turn limit our chances of success. Ellis (1991) outlined the ABC model of behaviour which clearly sets out this idea:

A   the activating event (or antecedent) –a situation that is prompting irrational behaviour
B   the beliefs about the event
C   the consequences of the event (the negative feelings experienced)

Ellis suggests that it is not the event itself that is the cause of negative emotions but the way in which it is interpreted – the irrational belief about it – and it is this we need to manage if we want to respond more positively. There are two key strategies to help change automatically negative or pessimistic thinking – distraction and disputation.

Distraction is probably the easiest of these to achieve and a simple strategy is to schedule in 'thinking time'. If something is bothering you, simply commit the details to paper, then schedule a time to think about it. This strategy cuts the 'niggling' thoughts and emotions off in their prime. They have not been ignored because they have been committed to paper, but they have not been allowed to hijack current activities. The likelihood is that by the time the scheduled time arrives, thinking around the event will have become a little more rational.

A similar strategy is the 'worry decision tree' (Butler *et al.*, 2018). This strategy provides a structure for directing attention away from worry and towards useful, practical activities. In doing so it allows the focus to be on things that can be immediately changed, making the overall concerns less overwhelming. The starting point is to note any concerns then ask the question 'Is there anything I can do about this?' If the answer is 'yes' then make a list of simple actions to complete. If the answer is 'no' then stop worrying and distract yourself. The second step is to ask yourself is there is anything you can do at this moment. If the answer is 'yes' then do it now. Then stop worrying and distract yourself. If the answer is 'no' plan what you could do and when. Then stop worrying and distract yourself.

The first two strategies are distraction techniques. Now we should consider the even more powerful disputation strategies. You are already aware of what ABC stands for – adding two more letters to this creates a framework for disputing irrational beliefs. ABCDE stands for

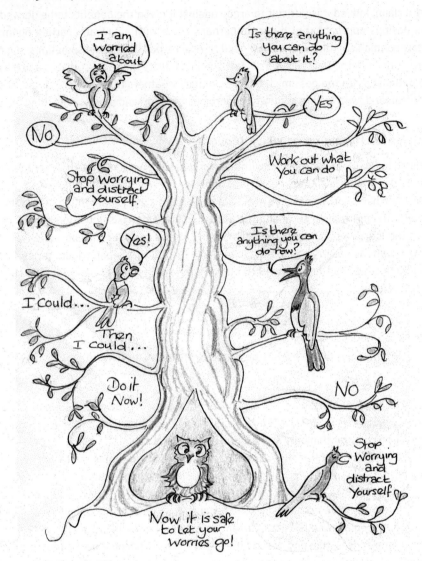

Figure 5.4 Worry decision tree

Antecedent (or activating event), Belief(s), Consequences, Disputation (dispute the beliefs), Energisation (be aware of feelings as you successfully deal with negative beliefs). The ABCDE strategy simply requires creating a record of an event using each of the headings and taking into account three factors:

- What is the evidence for the assumption I might be making?
- Are there any alternative assumptions?
- What are the implications of making this assumption?

For example:

Activating event – I wasn't invited to contribute a chapter to an edited book one of my colleagues is putting together.

Belief – My colleague thinks my work isn't good enough to be included in his book. My work must be poor compared to other colleagues (who have been invited to contribute).

Consequence – I feel upset that this is how my work is viewed. I am beginning to question whether or not I should do any more research or writing.

Disputation – I wasn't invited to contribute a chapter but is there any evidence that it is because of the quality of my work? It may simply be that my research doesn't fit with the overall theme? It is possible that my colleague is giving others the opportunity to publish and doesn't think I need this support? I probably don't need to do this.

Energisation – I don't feel upset about this now. Actually, I can see that there are many reasons why this happened and it isn't useful to dwell on it too much. I need to put my energies into my research!

Reframing is another method to disputing unhelpful beliefs and aiding the process of change. Based on the idea that we have a tendency to organise thinking into mental 'pigeon holes' which lead to habitual patterns of thinking, reframing offers a different way of looking at events. There are two types of reframes:

Context reframes where we might think about another context in which a given behaviour might be positive or useful. For example, a colleague always presents objections in team meetings – this is time-consuming and can come across as challenging. However, if the context were changed, and this happened within an explorative working group, the behaviour might be considered useful as it presented different perspectives. Content/meaning reframes relate to when we want to change the meaning we are giving to something, in a similar way as the ABCDE approach. In both cases the idea is to change the way of thinking about something and question prompts to help with this include:

- What else could this mean?
- How else could I describe this situation?
- What is the positive intent or value in this behaviour?
- Is there a larger frame in which the behaviour might have a positive value?

Chapter reflections

In this chapter we have considered the potential for reflection to become a negative process which can lead to forms of rumination, self-flagellation and negative spirals – psychological dynamite (Brookfield, 1990). The links between thoughts, beliefs and actions have been reinforced, with a particular focus on learning to think positively as well as pragmatically by building acceptance and openness to vulnerability within the reflective cycle. We have also considered a range of strategies which could be used to diffuse the dynamite and create space for more objective thought.

References

Brookfield, S. (1990) *Becoming a Critically Reflective Teacher*. San-Francisco, CA: Jossey-Bass.

Brown, B. (2012) *Daring Greatly: How the Courage to Be Vulnerable Transforms the Way We Live, Love, Parent and Lead*. Now York, NY: Gotham.

Brown, B. (2015) *Rising Strong*. London: Vermillion.

Burns, D. D. (2020) *Feeling Great, The Revolutionary New Treatment for Depression and Anxiety*. Eau Clair, WI: PESI.

Butler, G., Grey, N., & Hope, T. (2018) *Managing Your Mind – The Mental Fitness Guide* (3rd ed.). Oxford: Oxford University Press.

Ellis, A. (1991) 'The revised ABC's of rational-emotive therapy (RET)'. *Journal of Rational-Emotive and Cognitive-Behavior Therapy*, 9(3): 139-172.

Eurich, T. (2018) *Insight – How to Success by Seeing Yourself Clearly*. London: Pan Books.

Frankl, V. (2004) *Man's Search for Meaning*. New York, NY: Random House.

Goleman, D. (1996) *Emotional Intelligence: Why it Can Matter More Than IQ*. London: Bloomsbury.

Grant, A. M., Franklin, J., & Langford, P. (2002) 'The Self-Reflection and Insight Scale: A New Measure of Private Self-Consciousness'. *Social Behavior and Personality: An International Journal*, 30(8): 821-836.

Harrington, R., & Loffredo, D. A. (2010) 'Insight, Rumination, and Self-Reflection as Predictors of Well-Being'. *The Journal of Psychology*, 145(1): 39–57. doi: 10.1080/00223980.2010.528072.

Kubler-Ross, E. (2005) *On Grief and Grieving, Finding the Meaning of Grief through the Five Stages of Loss*. London: Simon & Schuster Ltd.

Luft, J., & Ingham, H. (1955) 'The Johari Window, a Graphic Model of Interpersonal Awareness'. In *Proceedings of the Western Training Laboratory in Group Development*. Los Angeles, CA: University of California.

Rogers, C. R. (1961) *On Becoming a Person – A Therapist's View of Psychotherapy*. New York, NY: Haughton Mifflin Company.

Seligman, M. (2006) *Learned Optimism* (2nd ed.). London: Nicholas Brealey Publishing.

Figure 6.1 Chapter mindmap

6 Tools for reflection

If the doors of perception were cleansed every thing would appear to man as it is, Infinite. For man has closed himself up, till he sees all things thro' narrow chinks of his cavern.

(William Blake, 1975, plate 14, xxii)

The importance of recognising habitual thinking, of challenging our perceptions with a critical eye and of seeking other perspectives has been a key thread of this book – and all of that is captured nicely in two sentences of Blake's *The Marriage of Heaven and Hell*. There is little doubt that developing the reflective habit can be illuminating both for professional practice, and for life and to develop this we do need to consider some practical tools that can help to 'cleanse the doors of perception'. The busyness of modern life has created a whirlwind of activity that can be difficult to slow down, and whilst we may well understand the benefits of regular and structured reflection, it is possible that we have forgotten how to go about this. In this chapter we will consider some of the barriers to reflection and look at a range of tools that will build upon the 5- and 10-minutes strategies included in each of the chapters.

Mary understood the power of taking time to reflect on life. She had learnt this at an early age as being part of a large family meant there was always some sort of drama going on in the house where she grew up. As she was the youngest, she was rarely included in any conversation so really had to make her own mind up about what was going on. Reading took her away from her family's drama to different places, different families, different ways of being. She often used this to inform her own thinking and learnt that she had developed the skill of seeing situations from a range of perspectives. The process was a natural one for her, and she actually looked forward to committing her thoughts to paper. There was something quite therapeutic about seeing the words fill the page.

Now that Mary was a teacher she could share that skill with others. Better still, her students were adults embarking on careers in social work, which meant that they had to develop reflective practice – it was an important part of their role. Mary had relished sharing her own ideas about reflection, and they had explored theories together and considered models to structure the initial reflections – they were ready. So. . . . She

DOI: 10.4324/9781003056812-7

was puzzled by the conversations she was having with many of the students which normally went along the lines of:

'I don't know how to do my journal.'

'Well as we discussed, the format is up to you. Maybe start by looking at one of the models we discussed.'

'Yes, I get that . . . but what should I write?'

'How about writing your thoughts and feelings about what has happened in your placement?'

'OK . . . but what should I write about? There isn't anything in the assessment outcomes that says what you are looking for . . . and how many words do I need?

This scenario is not unusual and I suspect many teachers have had similar conversations with their students – I know I have, many times. In day-to-day life we are so used to being constrained by standards, policies and specific guidelines that it can be really difficult to take charge of our own thoughts. It seems that even our thinking needs to be structured in such a way that it achieves a specific objective. This can create a barrier to reflection as the focus is on the end goal, the outcome of an assessment or the production of evidence for professional competence.

Barriers to reflection

Before looking at some tools to enhance reflection, it would be useful to explore a few of the barriers. Recognising barriers helps us to establish any blocks to effective reflection and a first step is to remove or at least to diminish them in order to create some space for our thoughts. Barriers to reflection may be defined as internal and external factors which influence our ability to reflect (Boud & Walker, 1993). Internal barriers might be things like previous experiences or presuppositions underpinning beliefs, very similar to the habitual ways of thinking we have discussed in previous chapters. External barriers are likely to come from the environment or other people and relate to environmental or cultural factors. The following outlines some of the most likely barriers reflective practitioners experience in their quest to find a reflective path.

Focussing on outcome rather than process

As illustrated by Mary's story, oftentimes people are so focussed on outcomes, they don't really consider the process. This is understandable as there are so many pressures to evidence our practice, both as students and as practitioners. This can have the impact of driving effort towards evidence building rather than towards thinking about our professional role.

Work or team cultures

An idea popularised by motivation speaker Jim Rohn is that 'you are the average of the 5 people you spend the most time with'. This is based on the power of influence and the idea that spending time with positive people who help you achieve your goals is a step to success. Whilst there is some truth in this, we also need to remember that we don't always choose the people we spend a lot of time with. At work, we may well be in teams with people we have very little in common with but who still have a significant influence on how we carry out day-to-day activities – even when we aren't aware of it. Groupthink is a psychological term used to describe how individuals attempt to achieve harmony by 'fitting in' (McCauley, 1989). Driven by a desire for cohesiveness and to be a part of the 'in-group', this creates a tendency to avoid conflict by conforming to accepted practice. The danger of course is that high levels of groupthink lead to less critical evaluation and produce a sense of unjustified certainty that the right decision has been made. In the long term this could mean avoiding creative approaches and embedding acknowledged and sometimes ineffective practice. Not only does this affect how we do things, it affects how we think about them so has a significant impact on reflective practice. You can see this easily in the way that others use language – when words become tangible things that cannot be questioned and groups almost create their own language around the practice that has been absorbed by the group as a whole. A typical example from my work is the term 'stretch and challenge' used by Ofsted (Office for Standards in Education) to describe how teaching can be made more challenging for learners. 'Stretch' and 'challenge' are both verbs – we may want to set up a lesson in order to stretch a learner's thinking or to challenge their current perceptions. But the two words together have become a noun in common parlance and seem to have evolved into a conjoined entity never to be separated, for example, 'think about your stretch-and-challenge,' as if it is a noun – a thing like a lesson plan or a teaching resource and something that we all understand without question. In NLP theory the term 'nominalisation' is used to describe the process of turning verbs into nouns in ways which limit actions because they turn contestable ideas into things which we assume everyone understands and therefore are no longer questioned.

Consider the following words – What do they mean to you?

Communication

Relationship

Love

Success

Leadership

Then think about how easy (or difficult) it is to have different interpretations of these words.

What impact does the way we use and interpret words have on our thinking and our actions?

Surveillance

Organisation cultures do vary, as do the microcultures within professions. In some professional roles there are high levels of surveillance whereby quality measures have a focus on observing and commenting on professional activity. Where this activity is concentrated, taking time out to think about and critique your practice is much more difficult. Not only do we feel the need to be doing things in expected ways, there is also more pressure to be seen to be constantly busy. There are some links here to Michel Foucault's idea of the Panopticon, which is a surveillance tower in a prison environment (Foucault, 1977). Although it is not possible for the singular guard in the surveillance tower to observe what all prisoners are doing at all times, the prisoners don't actually know that, so self-regulate their activities. The idea is based on the connection between knowledge and power and: 'reaches into the very grain of individuals, touches their bodies and inserts itself into their actions and attitudes, their discourses, learning processes and everyday lives' (Foucault, 1980: 30).

Environment

Culture does have a significant impact on our working environment, but we also need to consider the environment itself. If you work in a busy open plan office, it is very difficult to find the headspace for reflection. The comings and goings of other people will inevitably create a disturbance. Some people are more immune to this than others and are able to zone out the noise and activity just by putting on headphones. This is not so easy for others and it may be necessary to find an alternative space for reflection.

Motivation

I hope, after reading previous chapters that the importance of reflection is evident, but even if you clearly understand the benefits, sometimes it can be difficult to prioritise. When deadlines are piling up and colleagues are demanding your time, creating space for reflection can seem less important. Thinking about our work probably doesn't seem quite as important as actually doing it. The key here is to keep the process simple and short – 15 or 20 minutes out of your time is going to make very little difference to achieving your deadlines but might make all the difference to gaining some clarity of thought.

Self

Sometimes we are our own biggest barrier to effective reflection. It can be very difficult to be objective about the things that happen and about our own actions. In Chapter 4 we discussed the importance of critical reflection to help avoid using reflection as a form of confirmation bias, justifying our actions and confirming current beliefs. One reason we are all susceptible to this is lack of emotional literacy. This is an aspect of emotional intelligence (Salovey & Mayer, 1990) and could be described as our ability to express our feelings by recognising and naming emotions as well as our capacity to actively listen to and empathize with others. If you have grown up in a culture where discussing feelings is not encouraged, developing emotional literacy can be a challenge. We are often not specific about naming emotions and will be comfortable expressing some emotions but not others. For some people expressing anger or fear might be very difficult, for others it is the expression of joy or love that is problematic. In either case this can lead to not acknowledging or even deliberately blocking our feelings.

Similarly, when reflecting on feelings we may find that we justify them rather than explore them. For example, rather than saying 'I feel judged' and subsequently exploring the reasons for this, we might say 'I feel that they are judging me because . . . ' Although that is a simple difference, the former will lead to an explorative thought trail, the second is simply a decision made, no further reflection required!

Adil understood the importance of self-image – he had spent years refining his own and it was paying off. All of those early morning trips to the gym, missing out on nights out with friends so that he could save for a nicer suit, a better car . . . now he felt like he had finally arrived. He always looked good, he had a great job and he was confident that he was on the road to real success. His boss was always telling him what an asset he was to the team.

The only fly in the ointment was the other people he worked with. They were always joking around and making fun of each other. They didn't seem to care about their appearance and gave the general impression that the office was a place for joviality. They weren't as serious about or as good at their jobs as him and they knew it. Maybe that's why they didn't like hearing about his success? One or two of them had even been quite rude and questioned his expertise, and for some reason this was really bothering him. He knew it shouldn't, but it did. He hated to admit it, but when he was at home he felt really hurt by the comments and sometimes just wanted to curl up and hide under the duvet. The negative thoughts were disturbing his sleep, and he couldn't have his routine upset like that.

A friend had suggested that he try keeping a reflective journal to try to explore some of his thoughts. Apparently, this would help him to clarify things – but what was there to clarify? He knew he was right and that others were wrong – what was the point of reflecting on that? All he had to do was to continue to give the right impression to the others and that meant being fit and healthy, dressing well and showing his most confident self at work. After all, image was everything. Everyone knew that.

He just wished he could stop thinking about the things people had said. He hated the way it was making him feel. The negative comments pecking away at his brain like angry birds. He was unable to calm them, and it was exhausting.

All of Life's a stage!

How important is it to create the right impression? How often are we occupied with thoughts of what others might think of us? In Adil's case his professional persona is so important it is impacting on his home life. This seems extreme, but how unusual is it really? How many of us have come home from work feeling like we have been run over by a bus when all that has happened is we have had a less than satisfactory interaction with a colleague or two? Goffman's dramaturgical theory is based on the idea that life is a never-ending play in which we are all actors. (Goffman, 1956) From birth, we are thrust onto the stage of life, in which we act out a number of roles in the company of others. We have many roles linked to work, family and community and each of them has expectations attached to it. Goffman also recognised different stages in our interactions and suggested that the *front stage* was where we were likely to be seen by the world, whereas the *backstage* represented aspects of who we really are. It is backstage where we are likely to feel accepted and not have the pressure of trying to fit in with others' expectations of us.

Goffman suggests that actors are constantly occupied with impression management – in that they are concerned with managing the impression that others have of them. In such cases the behaviour presented will be the behaviour that is likely to be that which is considered acceptable in a certain situation. For Adil, this was about looking the part and presenting what he viewed as a confident image in the workplace, but his colleagues had different ideas about how office interactions should play out. Clearly the rules about appropriate behaviour in the workplace were different for the actors on this stage.

Dramaturgical theory is based on the idea that behaviour is closely linked to context, therefore certain behaviours are considered appropriate in certain contexts and not in others. This suggests that an individual's identity is not something that is stable but is constantly remade in different interactions. When these identities are more of a blur, or perhaps when one identity underpins most of our actions, then we may not view events in context but see them as a reflection of other people's perceptions of us. In Adil's case, his professional image and the impression he was making in the workplace underpinned most of his actions so it was difficult for him to see that his colleagues' actions were just the role they played at work. To them, the interaction was likely to be insignificant, whereas to Adil it presented something that made him question his self-image. If people don't interact with us in the way that we expect, then judgements about who is 'right' and 'wrong' are likely to ensue. Adil's decision was very clear . . . he was right and his colleagues were wrong, therefore he would continue to do what he had been doing and would most likely get exactly the same result.

5-minute reflection strategy – judgement reframe

Think of a recent event where you have made a firm judgement about someone or something. For example, in the case study, Adil had judged his colleagues for not taking their work seriously, labelling them as less competent than himself. You may have judged someone on how they dealt with something, on their appearance, on the way they spoke to you . . . First write down your initial judgement without editing it. Then reframe it by asking yourself 'What else could this mean?', 'What purpose did this behaviour serve?'

Using the judgement reframe strategy is a useful way of considering alternative perspectives. By writing down our initial thoughts and judgements we are acknowledging them and then by asking the question 'What else could this mean?' we are forced to consider alternative perspectives. Finally, when asking the question, 'What purpose did this behaviour serve?', we must consider the positive intention behind the behaviour, which helps our over-all understanding in context and may help to reframe our initial thoughts.

Tools for reflection

There is no single way of structuring your reflections. In fact some might suggest you don't structure them at all and allow the process to lead you. However, whilst there is some sense in that, it isn't helpful to the new reflective practitioner who might need some practical guidance to get started. The following strategies outline a range of ways in which reflective thought can be structured. They can be used as a starting point until you find your own way forward or for the times when you feel a little stuck and simply need a different approach.

Creating headspace

An oft-cited reason for not reflecting is that we just don't have the headspace to do it. There are so many thoughts, ideas and plans occupying our minds the idea of inflicting even more thinking might seem superfluous. The human mind is rarely quiet but as outlined in Chapter 4, there is a difference between the automatic thinking linked to familiar and often inconse-quential things and deliberate thinking – what Dewey referred to as 'thinking well' (Dewey, 1910). In order to think well, we need to find a way of slowing down the omnipresent chatter.

Freud (in Strachey *et al.*, 1978) believed that the mind had three parts – the conscious, pre-conscious and unconscious – and used the metaphor of an iceberg to illustrate this. The tip of the iceberg, above the water line, represents the conscious mind that deals with thoughts,

Figure 6.2 Conscious-unconscious

understandings and the memories we acknowledge. These are the things that occupy our automatic thinking – our day-to-day chatter. The preconscious mind exists just below the surface of the water. You can see the outline and are aware of it but need to make an effort to access it. Information such as phone numbers or bank account details are stored here, not in day-to-day use but accessible when you need them. The unconscious mind is represented by the large mass hidden beneath the water line, apparently innocent until hit by a passing ship! This represents things hidden from conscious awareness but which still influence thoughts, behaviours and actions.

Freud's view on the conscious and unconscious mind are well documented. In particular the notion that it is the unconscious mind that holds the key to our personalities with the conscious mind being the babysitter, managing what is acceptable and not so acceptable to think about. He wasn't the only one with this view. According to Jung (1954), 'The unconscious mind of man sees correctly even when the conscious reason is blind and impotent' (page 27). If this is the case, wouldn't it be great to be able to tap into the unconscious mind and unravel all the mysteries of life? There are many strategies recommended to help you do this – for example, hypnotherapy – and their effectiveness, or not, is a matter for personal judgement. However, what the various approaches do have in common is the implementation of strategies to slow down our thinking and switching focus from the constant chatter, starting with the development of mindfulness.

Mindfulness is based on a general awareness cultivated by paying particular attention to things. It is something we do deliberately with a focus on attention to the present moment. It doesn't have to be a full meditation but does focus on awareness of thoughts and feelings and the avoidance of any judgement. It can be practiced in different ways from simply paying attention to breathing to more formal meditations. A simple strategy for developing mindfulness might be:

- Find a moment to pause your activities
- Direct your attention to your breathing
- Try to slow breathing – try the 7-11 technique (breathe in for the count of 7, breathe out for the count of 11)
- Focus on immediate feelings
- Accept thoughts without judgement

Mindfulness leads to mind wandering and potentially the surfacing of unconscious associations. At the very least it takes your mind away from the habitual chatter of daily thoughts.

Metaphor and stories

Throughout history, stories have played a significant role in learning. They capture our attention and can present nuggets of insight we might not otherwise encounter. In a similar way, metaphors provide symbolic representations that may alter perceptions or help us to develop deeper insight. Both metaphor and stories have the bonus of being indirect, which means they are both objective and contextually meaningful. The story might be about someone else, but we are able to transfer its meaning to our own context and better still, because it is not about us, we can do so without any judgement. Stories also have the power to create dissonance by introducing contradictory ideas that stretch our thinking. To illustrate this, I want to share a story:

> One evening an old farmer was walking along a country lane. He looked into a field and saw a group of young women bathing naked in a pond. The women noticed him at about the same time as he noticed them.
>
> One woman shouted, 'We're not coming out till you leave.'
>
> The farmer replied, 'Oh, I'm not here to watch you ladies swimming naked, or running around in the meadow with nothing on.
>
> I'm just here to feed the alligator.'

(Owen, 2011: 103)

Creating dissonance might also be described as introducing a few alligators. It grabs our attention and provides an alternative perspective. Stories, metaphors, allegorical tales can help us connect information in a variety of ways and are a great source of inspiration. In reflective practice, they can be used to provide a range of perspectives, to help clarify thoughts and to contextualise things which initially seem unconnected. You simply need to start a collection of stories and access them whenever you need inspiration.

Asking others

It is very easy to be absorbed by our own reflections, so much so that we struggle to see different perspectives. Another way of introducing a few alligators is by asking for some feedback from others and using this as a basis for reflection. This can be framed as a peer observation whereby someone is invited to observe your practice and record their thoughts about it. A simple tool to structure this is to use the 'stolen goods' format, which is a framework for constructive feedback. This requires a format with only two headings: 'things I would steal from you' to highlight aspects of your practice the observer would like to model and 'things I would offer you' to outline some suggestions for improvements. This approach supports observation of practice which is less focussed on judgements (in the form of grades or labels) and has a focus on objective and developmental feedback.

Journalling

A journal (sometimes referred to as a reflective log) is a record of events alongside thoughts and feelings about them. Journals might be considered a personal adventure (Bolton, 2001) and are one of the main cornerstones of reflective practice. They can take any format: handwritten, typewritten, separate notes in a scrapbook, whatever appeals to the writer – this is an important point as journals should be for the writer's eyes only. This level of privacy enables far more free expression, even if you choose to share some of your reflections with others.

What should you write about? As illustrated by the first case study, it can be really difficult to start your journal if you don't know what you should be writing about but in truth, there is no right or wrong with a journal. It is very personal to you, so you can write about whatever is on your mind. If it is a real struggle to get started, you could go back to the models outlined in Chapter 2 and use some of the prompts from there. Ultimately, a journal should be about questioning, exploring and analysing what you do, and this will include investigating what you think and how you feel. It may be written in any style, and it is likely that your style will evolve. You may even embellish your journal with thoughts borrowed from others by using excepts, quotes, poems or images.

A few tips to get started:

- Write for yourself initially as this will aid free expression – you can always share your thoughts later if you choose to.
- Remember to include dates – you are likely to forget this, and it may be important when you go back to your reflections.
- Try a range of writing styles to find a good fit. A descriptive style will allow you to record an event, an exploratory style will prompt questions, a critical style will support analysis. You can even take a creative style if it is easier to express your thoughts in this way.
- If your journal entry is focussed on a particular concern you would like to resolve, avoid being too solution-focussed – use the journal to think things through. Jumping to a solution very quickly may mean you haven't explored potential actions in enough detail.
- Try to find a regular slot for writing. Do this at the same time of day or on the same day of the week, depending on how often you choose to write.

creative writing

Sometimes finding the right words to express ourselves is a struggle. Particularly when we are reflecting on emotions. Committing our intimate thoughts to a well-constructed sentence may not be possible, let alone desirable, yet we may be able to express them in a poem, a letter or a piece of creative writing. Different genres provide a choice of outlets for expressing thoughts and feelings and allow us to represent a range of voices. This is illustrated nicely in Bolton (2001) in the reflections of a Doctor, expressed poetically by writing a letter to patients:

> I am listening, really I am.
>
> I have to be honest, though – sometimes it's hard to pay attention. If my focus seems to shift away from you to the clock or the door, or the computer, please don't think it's because I don't care.
>
> Let me tell you something, my friend. I've got problems, too. Sometimes my problems are bigger than yours and I'm hanging on by my fingernails. But I'm the one with the desk and the prescription pad.
>
> And what am I doing while you struggle to explain yourself to me?
>
> I'm holding myself together, is what I'm doing. So make the most of me.
>
> (page 158)

By using a different genre we have the option of removing ourselves from the scene, which is helpful when we want to reflect on something that is difficult to express.

10-minute Reflection Strategy - A Letter to a Stranger

Select the most difficult event of the week. Then write a letter to a stranger outlining what happened, what you thought and felt about the event and what impact it has had on you. Remember the stranger has no significance in your life other than being the recipient of your letter.

By writing a letter about a difficult event, we put ourselves in the position of thinking carefully about sequence and need to express thoughts with clarity, which in turn can aid objectivity. There is also a purpose in this being a letter to a stranger . . . if we don't have a relationship, we have no role in that person's life and are not concerned with impression management, therefore, our description is likely to be honest and will not be influenced by any expectations of the relationship.

Drawing

In Chapter 4 I suggested that the use of a storyboard as a strategy for enhancing critical thinking. The use of drawing in a more general way is also helpful in that it brings about an altered consciousness, as suggested by Edwards: 'In drawing, you will delve deeply into a part of your mind often obscured by endless details of daily life. From this experience you will develop your ability to perceive things freshly in their totality, to see underlying patterns and possibilities for new combinations' (2001: 6). By becoming engrossed in the activity it is possible to envisage creative solutions to issues as we are putting the conscious mind to work on an activity, allowing the unconscious mind the freedom to roam and maybe deposit a helpful nugget or two into consciousness.

Finding your own way

The tools for reflection outlined in this chapter are simply suggestions to provide prompts. They are by no means strategies that must be followed. We all experience times when we feel a little stuck, and my personal experience is that a change of approach can be very helpful in moving past the blocks. When I become stuck, I tend to draw my thoughts, sometimes in storyboard form, sometimes as mindmaps and sometimes just as a random collection of things. Becoming focussed on the drawing, rather than my thoughts certainly helps to change perspective. Anecdotal evidence from colleagues suggests that changing the format of their writing can be helpful, for example, trying to apply a different genre to something they are struggling with. So long as the strategy helps to move things forward, it doesn't really matter what approach is taken and the important thing is that you find your own path. It is your reflective journey, so you need to create your own map as following someone else's may not lead you to the right destination.

Chapter reflections

In this chapter we have considered potential barriers to reflection and discussed a range of tools that can be used to overcome any blocks we may experience. Whilst it is important to remember that reflection is a personal thing and should be informed by your own ideas, it is also worth remembering that we all get stuck at times and sometimes need a change of direction in order to move forwards.

References

Blake, W. (1975) *The Marriage of Heaven and Hell, Oxford Paperback*. Oxford: Oxford University Press.

Bolton, G. (2001) *Reflective Practice, Writing and Professional Development*. London: Paul Chapman Publishing Ltd.

Boud, D., & Walker, D. (1993) 'Barriers to Reflection on Experience'. In D. Boud *et al.* (eds.), *Using Experience for Learning*. Buckingham: SHRE and Open University Press.

Dewey, J. (1910) *How We Think*. Boston, MA: D C Heath & Co.

Edwards, B. (2001) *The New Drawing on the Right Side of the Brain*. London: Harper Collins.

Foucault, M. (1977) *Discipline and Punishment: The Birth of the Prison*. New York, NY: Vintage Books.

Foucault, M. (1980) *Power/Knowledge: Selected Interviews and Other Writings, 1972-1977*. New York, NY: Pantheon.

Freud, S. (1978) *The Standard Edition of the Complete Psychological Works of Sigmund Freud. Volume V (1900-1) Interpretation of Dreams II and On Dreams* (J. Strachey, A. Freud, 1895-1982, C. L. Rothgeb, 1925, A. Richards, eds.), Scientific Literature Corporation. London: Hogarth Press.

Goffman, E. (1956) *The Presentation of Self in Everyday Life*. New York, NY. Doubleday.

Jung, C. (1954) *Answer to Job*. London: Routledge and Kegan Paul.

McCauley, C. (1989). 'The Nature of Social Influence in Groupthink: Compliance and Internalization'. *Journal of Personality and Social Psychology*, 57(2): 250-260. https://doi.org/10.1037/0022-3514.57.2.250.

Owen, N. (2011) *More Magic of Metaphor, Stories for Leaders, Influencers, Motivators and Spiral Dynamics Wizards*. Wales: Crown House Publishing Ltd.

Salovey, P., & Mayer, J. D. (1990) 'Emotional Intelligence'. *Imagination, Cognition, and Personality*, 9: 185-211.

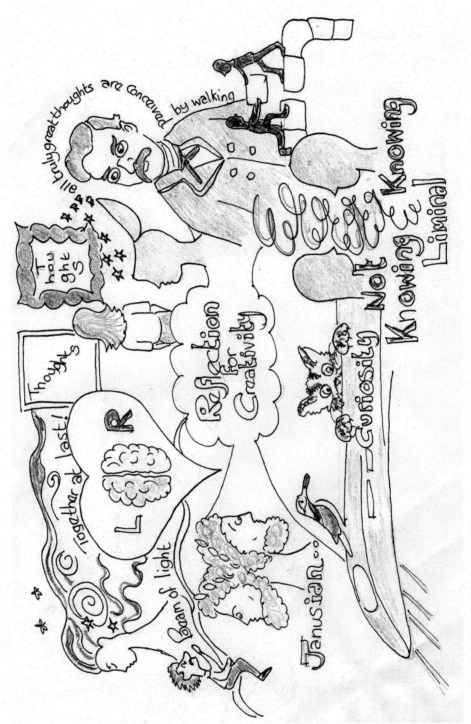

Figure 7.1 Chapter mindmap

7 Reflection for creativity

Reflection often focusses on issues in our practice and as a result can be dominated by the need to find solutions. Many of the models of reflection outlined in Chapter 3 encourage us to do just that by logging concerns, making sense of them and then considering appropriate action. As suggested previously, models have their uses, but they can also become mechanistic – the use of cycles and actions most certainly lead the focus to finding a specific solution for a specific issue. But what if reflection had another purpose? What if it also provided fertile ground for creative thought, helped us not only to think differently but to see things in completely new ways? In this chapter we will consider the ways in which reflective practice can enhance creative thinking and provide us with a range of new perspectives, ideas and creative imaginings.

What is creativity?

Creativity is a powerful term, often associated with a 'special few' who have an ability that we recognise as creative, such as art, music or literature – but what does it really mean? According to Robinson (2017) if we take creativity in its broadest sense we could apply it to many of the day-to-day activities carried out at home and in work and in doing so, recognise the creative capacity of every individual. By thinking differently about our talents and abilities we also open ourselves up to being even more creative. Robinson's key argument is that society, and in particular education, have taught us to focus on what might be considered scientific subjects and we have neglected the arts in favour of this, thereby relegating creativity to the domain of the creative elite – those people who have made something that we categorise as creative. Although the importance of creativity is acknowledged in Western society, we certainly have a focus on things considered to be scientific or logical. As Samples (1976) suggests, we favour the rational mind over the metaphoric and, quoting Einstein, he suggests that in doing this we may be limiting our potential: 'Einstein called the intuitive or metaphoric mind a sacred gift. He added that the rational mind was a faithful servant. It is paradoxical that in the context of modern life we have begun to worship the servant and defile the divine' (1976: 26).

Creativity is often viewed as a process linked to the generation of new or original ideas and this is probably why many people say they are not creative. Making reference to the well-known research carried out by Roger Sperry in the 60s, they might even say they are 'left-brained' to indicate a dominance of logic or analytical thought. (in Robinson, 2017)

DOI: 10.4324/9781003056812-8

Sperry's seminal research into the structure and function of the brain concluded that the two hemispheres of the brain fulfilled different but complementary functions. The left favouring things such as logic, number skills and reasoning and the right things such as imagination, creativity and emotion. People often see themselves as left-brained or right-brained depending on what is dominant but this idea has been disputed. Nielson *et al.* (2013) suggests that whilst functions of hemisphere may be different, this has more to do with how they process information. For example, the left-side of the brain may process the details of a visual object whilst the right takes in the overall shape. The left processes literal meaning in language whilst the right is able to decode indirect meaning. This suggests that both sides of the brain work together, and people don't have a dominant hemisphere.

Anni was retraining as a teacher whilst also managing her day job in the police force. She was a capable and conscientious student, always striving to do better. Anni was beginning to get concerned about her next teaching observation. She knew that she was a competent teacher because she was very organised and very good a managing groups of learners, but she also knew that her observer would be looking for something more than that. Something a little beyond the ordinary. When she discussed this concern with her tutor, Anni's main worry was that it was her lack of creativity that would let her down: 'The problem is I am very left-brained, I really struggle to come up with creative ideas.'

When we say we are not creative, what is usually true is that we are not used to using our creative capacity – or that we don't recognise it when we do. It could also be said that through inculcated messages of right and wrong, good and bad we are taught to conform to generally accepted norms. In Anni's story the right way to do things was ingrained in her day-to-day working life. She was used to following procedures and rules. She very often didn't have to think beyond that as there was a written policy or set protocol for almost every aspect of the work. When it came to her teaching, she had experienced a little more freedom in how she structured lessons and whilst this was a joy to her it was also a worry. She wasn't used to thinking creatively and (in her mind) she wasn't any good at it. As suggested in chapter one, our world-view is also influenced by a range of factors, and we could argue that the same can be said for creativity (Robinson, 2017). We only need to look to children for examples of this, as Picasso is often credited with saying: 'all children are artists, the problem is staying an artist when you grow up' (pablopicasso.org online). At a young age children think in divergent ways, using their imagination to make sense of their world; yet when they grow and become educated, this is very often diminished. The same can happen in the workplace, and Anni's story isn't that unusual. In truth, the main thing impacting on Anni's ability to be creative was the way she viewed herself.

The reality is that coming up with completely new ideas is difficult and probably unrealistic. When you think about it, how many things are completely new? Works of art are generally based on aspects of life; there was something already in existence that provided the inspiration. Perhaps creativity has more to do with our ability to connect things, to generate new meaning, than it does with producing an aesthetically pleasing artefact such as a painting or a sculpture?

diffusion of innovation

Innovation isn't about creating entirely new things but has more to do with how we adapt what is already familiar in new and innovative ways. The theory of diffusion of innovation describes how an idea gains momentum over a period of time and spreads through the social system. (Rogers, 2003) This theory is based on a model of social change and is focussed on how ideas are disseminated through social channels until they become a part of everyday conversation. In modern society it is very easy to see how this happens through the range of communication channels available to us. Just think about how quickly funny messages or video clips are spread via platforms such as WhatsApp or Facebook. When such ideas are adapted, they take on a new form and, in a sense, become a completely new innovation. This may seem like something of a cheat, but we could argue that truly original ideas are quite rare. When Leonardo Da Vinci was considering ideas about human flight, his drawings were based on bird flight. More recently, changes to the Japanese bullet trains were inspired by Kingfishers. The train's original design was burdened by sonic boom caused by changing air pressure. To resolve this, engineers took their inspiration from nature – they had noticed that Kingfishers travel between air and water with minimal splash, so the trains were remodelled with a long beak-shaped nose which significantly reduced the amount of noise they made and allowed them travel 10% faster. Many modern-day inventions have been based on Einstein's theories. For example, the laser pointer used in a variety of products today came out of an idea that Einstein had in 1917 when he was trying to understand how light interacted with matter. Creating a laser pointer is undoubtedly considered an important innovation, but whether the ideas was new or not is a matter of debate. According to Csikszentmihalyi (1996), creativity can be defined as 'any act, idea, or product that changes an existing domain or that transforms an existing domain into a new one' (1996: 28). This seems to recognise the importance of adaptation as a part of the process. Rather than thinking about creativity as a rare ability of the gifted elite, perhaps we need to reconsider our definition. As Robinson suggests, creativity encompasses three key things: imagination, the development of new ideas and the ways in which we put these new ideas into practice.

Thinking in opposites

Most people probably recognise the outcomes of creative thinking, such as works of art or literature, but how many of us recognise the process of creativity? How often are we aware of the creative things we do or the creative thoughts we might have . . . and if we are, do we understand the process sufficiently to replicate it, or is it something relegated to serendipity?

In formulating a theory about how human creativity transpires, Koestler put forward the term 'bisociation', which refers to the combination of an object or idea from two fields that are not normally considered to be related (Koestler, 1964). Koestler recognised the boundaries between very different fields of knowledge and questioned whether these boundaries could be more fluid than we think: 'Science is said to aim at Truth, Art at Beauty; but the criteria of Truth (such as verifiability and refutability) are not as clean and hard as we tend to believe, and the criteria of Beauty are, of course, even less so' (1964: 28).

This process has also been referred to as Janusian thinking (Rothenberg, 1971) based on the story of the Roman God Janus, who had two faces, each looking in the opposite direction. By imagining the two opposites – objects, contradictory ideas or concepts existing simultaneously – we are able to conceive a new idea developed from a symbiosis of the two.

5-minute reflection strategy – making connections

Select two unrelated objects within your house – for example, a cooking utensil and a product you use in your skincare routine. Without editing your ideas, write down any ways you can think of combining these two objects.

The purpose of this reflective strategy is to encourage divergent thinking. By removing familiar combinations, we are creating space for new ways of seeing things and have the potential to think about them in a completely different way. Divergent thinking is an important aspect of creativity as it may lead to new ideas but at the very least will open up a new avenue of thought.

Reflection to enhance the creative process

The previous reflection activity emphasises the importance of looking at the commonplace in different ways in order to generate creative insights, but what part does reflection play in this? As we have explored in previous chapters, thoughts and actions are habitual, and it is only by breaking these habits that we can begin to think differently. Reflective practice encourages us to analyse our thoughts, and in this process we are breaking them down in parts in order to form different combinations. It is a little like musical improvisation; we bring to it a range of 'sounds' and aim to blend these into something harmonious. If all instruments play different tunes at the same time this will likely result in an awful din, but when we step back and really listen to each one, we can pick out connections. The reflective process provides the space for the detailed analysis of parts, which then allows us to synthesise our ideas into a more harmonious whole. Through the process, and by using a range of different approaches to reflection, we also change our habitual patterns of thought and are able to tap into other sources of information using both the rational and intuitive parts of our brains.

One important aspect to consider is that creativity comes in many forms and functions in holistic ways. For example, dance is a kinaesthetic form of creativity yet relies on visual interpretation as well as music. Mathematics is often seen as an abstract skill based on logic, yet it has similarities to music in that both have a strong affinity to patterns. Analytical thought and creative thought do not necessarily fit into neat compartments and many great thinkers acknowledged this. Einstein, for example, is certainly recognised for his analytical mind, yet was a great advocate of imagination and was well known for using visualisation as a form of thought experiment to test out his theories. Thinking about creativity as a singular trait may not be helpful, as Robinson suggests it isn't a single ability: 'It thrives on the dynamism between different ways of thinking and being' (2017: 104).

the importance of imagination

Einstein's famous quote: 'Imagination is more important than knowledge' (Calaprice, 2011: 12) is often put forward as an example of the importance of creative thought, and as the quote suggests, Einstein was an advocate of the benefits of the imaginal: 'Knowledge is limited. Imagination encircles the world' (Ibid.). In his book (co-authored with Leopold Infeld) Einstein expresses the importance of imagination by comparing the work of the scientist with that of the detective and concludes that whilst both seek answers, the detective has the benefit of knowing the problem, in that he knows what crime has been committed. The scientist, on the other hand, must formulate his own crime: 'The formulation of a problem is often more essential than its solution, which may be merely a matter of experimental skill. To raise new questions, new possibilities, to regard old problems from a new angle, requires creative imagination and marks real advances in science' (Einstein & Infeld, 1938: 95).

Imagination and creativity are closely connected but are not the same thing. Imagination helps us to bring to mind things not experienced by our senses, and creativity is what helps us to put those things to work (Robinson, 2017). What is important about imagination is that through it we can experience things that have existed, do exist and even those that do not. Consider how the author creates a futuristic scene or how the artist paints an image of an unknown world and we have clear examples of this: 'Imagination enables you to step out of the here and now. You can revisit and review the past. You can take a different view of the present by putting yourself in the minds of others and can try to see with their eyes and feel with their hearts. In imagination you can anticipate many possible futures' (Robinson, 2017: 129).

10-minute Reflection Strategy – Sliding Doors

This strategy is based on the 1998 film of the same name in which a woman's love life and career are closely connected to whether or not she catches a specific train. As the film progresses, we see each story play out. The events that follow when she does catch the train, and a parallel tale which unfolds when she doesn't. Each story has some similarities but also very different outcomes.

Consider an event or opportunity, for example, a prospective new job that you are considering, a personal goal, or maybe something associated to a pertinent relationship. Using your imagination create a script with various options. What possible opportunities will present themselves? What potential hurdles might you come across? How does the story unfold in the different scripts?

The purpose of this strategy is to think through a range of possibilities. When considering a course of action this might help to test out potential options to see if they are a good fit for us. By creating a story, we are also extending our thinking beyond the issue itself and can test out the routes that feel right. Really letting our imagination run free is the key here – if we constrain it then we are likely to opt for the well-trodden path of familiarity and by default take similar actions which most likely result in similar outcomes.

Strategies for creative reflection

If we choose to reflect to generate creative ideas or simply to enhance our creative abilities, it is worth considering some specific strategies to facilitate this. Very often all we need to do is alter our path by approaching reflective practice in a different way, and here are ten strategies to try out:

1   *Seek paradoxical options* – if you have something in particular to reflect on, then consider a paradoxical option, something perhaps contradictory, which seems unreasonable or unlikely but in the right context it might make sense. For example, your department budget is overspent, and you need to find savings. A paradoxical option would be to spend more.

2   *Practice pattern recognition* – look for the patterns in nature, in biology, in behaviour, the world is built upon patterns, rhythms and cycles that play out time and time again. The aphorism 'history repeats itself' is based on this idea and is something that can be seen not only in world history but in our personal histories. According to Bates (1972) we are all parts of a system containing causal chains, by recognising patterns we also uncover connections which may develop new understandings.

3   *Map it* – mindmapping allows you to get lots of ideas on a single sheet of paper and to show connections between them. You can simply use words, but adding images provides the option of including things that you may not yet have words for. Mindmaps encourage free-flowing thoughts. We are not limiting the process by trying to construct full sentences or even produce something that is coherent. Simply get a sheet of paper and in the middle use a keyword or image to show the main theme. From this, branches reach out representing sub-themes and further images or sub-branches can be added to these. There are examples of my mindmaps at the beginning of each chapter – in this context they serve as an overview of the chapter content as well as a quick reference point, but I also use them to generate ideas.

4   *Walk* – Nietzsche understood the benefits of walking when he said: 'All truly great thoughts are conceived by walking.' Now it's official: 'Walking boosts creative ideation in real time and shortly after' (Opezzo & Schwartz, 2014: 1152). Running has a similar impact. The author Haruki Murakami, well-known for being a prolific writer, also runs every day (Murakami, 2014). This theory probably has more to do with being immersed in an activity which you carry out with unconscious competence so the same probably applies to cycling, swimming and other forms of consistent movement.

5   *Scrapbook* – reflection doesn't need to be words – it can involve any form of communication, but it is helpful to record it so that you can revisit some of the ideas. A scrap-

book is less linear than a written journal, as it can include a range of things, words of course but not necessarily always your own words; quotes, poems and songs are also relevant and provide inspiration for exploring ideas. You could also include more tactile things such as fabrics, so it has the benefit of being descriptive, visual and kinaesthetic. It is also possible to produce a digital version, which can include words, images, video clips and sound.

6   *Collaborate* - whilst reflection is usually viewed as a solo activity, it can be useful to talk to others as this offers the opportunity to test out ideas and gain a range of perspectives on them. Reflective discussions can be structured around meaningful topics, chosen by participants or can be less structured. The key aim is that it is a positive experience that allows all participants to share ideas and extend their thinking without judgement or the need to pinpoint a solution.

7   *Draw a roadmap* - this is a useful strategy for outlining significant events that may lead to deeper insights into our current state and potential direction, so it is a useful activity if we are not sure which direction to take. It involves drawing a roadmap, including significant dates, events or people. Events may be shown as twists and turns, bumps in the road, hill climbs or gentle meandering paths. The map shows that our past is behind us but has informed our direction and that our future is imagined but there are options in terms of the routes we take.

8   *Take a fantasy journey* - a scripted fantasy starts with a short relaxation exercise, such as deep breathing followed by some vague suggestions from which you construct the 'fantasy'. If you have ever been to a relaxation or yoga class, you will have experienced something similar at the end of the class. The idea is that individuals can enter a world of their own imagination, taking the fantasy to wherever they see fit and in doing so utilise their imagination to explore ideas, emotions or practice (Hall & Leech, 1990). The key to this is the use of 'artfully vague' language based on the work of Milton Erikson (Bandler, 2008). This is used to inspire change in thinking patterns, but change that is unique to the individual as the realisations come from within rather than from someone else. The language simply guides the journey, it doesn't direct it. There is an example of a simple script in the 5-minute reflection in this chapter.

9   *Create a storyboard* - storyboards are a useful tool for exploring ideas. They are simply drawings organised into a sequence. The idea is to focus on the story and where it takes you, rather than the images themselves, and explore ideas without being too concerned about how they are described. You can even download software to do this - although my view is that there is something to be gained by involving yourself in the kinaesthetic activity of drawing as this creates a sense of being absorbed by the task, a creative flow where you are fully immersed in the task (Csikszentmihalyi, 2008).

10 *Use a reframe* - as outlined in Chapter 2, we are all influenced by our frames of reference - sets of assumptions through which experiences are filtered so that we might make meaning from them. They can also create a sense of being 'stuck' in our thinking. Reframing, as outlined in Chapter 5, is a strategy we can use to highlight alternative ways of looking at things.

5-minute Reflection - Artfully Vague Fantasy

Read this passage at a relaxed pace and focus your attention inwards noticing your reactions to it.

As you sit back and relax, I wonder if you can imagine some restful, peaceful place? Begin to relax your body for this journey. Where is your journey taking you? What do you see? What can you hear? Paying attention to your breathing. What small things do you notice? Whilst you might be wondering which path to take, you might begin to get curious about your journey. As you begin to imagine a place where your mind is free to flow, your mind is now becoming more open to the idea of change, making the connections you have to make. As you meander along your chosen path you begin to notice . . .

Artfully vague language is intended to provide a trance like state that is individual, similar to that you might experience when involved in an activity you can complete with unconscious competence - something you do regularly that requires no direct thinking, for example walking, riding a bike or driving. The choice of language is deliberately vague so that no thoughts or ideas are imposed and the journey can be taken in any direction. The example here can of course be extended. It has been included to demonstrate the language style and is deliberately incomplete.

The power of stories

Stories can be powerful tools in generating creative thought. In chapter six we considered how they provide an indirect context into which we can transfer our own ideas or even explore issues that might be personal to us. Stories can be both objective, as they make no direct reference to us, but also personally meaningful because of the way we connect to them. They are powerful because they tap into our emotions and when we become immersed in a story, even though we know it is not real, we can feel emotion towards it. Stories also encourage us to visualise and stretch our imagination. Stories might also introduce some cognitive dissonance by throwing a few 'alligators' in our path - they can introduce ideas that might seem alien to us, thereby encouraging contemplation of alternative ideas.

Every culture has its stories, and over time stories take on a different significance. We turn to myths and fairy tales for wisdom and insight and absorb ideas when they are framed within the narrative of a story. Through stories we can reflect on our experiences, delve deeper into distant notions or explore completely new territory. A story can spark the imagination in powerful ways and plays an important role in shaping new ideas.

Curiosity and liminality

Curiosity could be described as the pursuit of new learning and the desire to fill gaps in our knowledge. When we are curious, we also have a willingness to explore new things, and we are motivated to learn. It is often thought of as a trait, something fixed which we either possess or don't, but curiosity is also a skill. It is something we can develop through practice by being open to new ideas, as articulated by the White Queen from *Alice's Adventures in Wonderland*: [Alice] 'There's no use trying,' she said. 'One can't believe impossible things.' 'I dare say you haven't had much practice,' said the Queen. 'When I was your age I always did it for half an hour a day. Why, sometimes I believed as many as six impossible things before breakfast' (Carroll, 1865). As suggested by this quote, enhanced curiosity brings with it less security in our knowledge, and through our new learning we may also be pushed to believing 'impossible things', which is not always a comfortable state.

Liminality describes a disorientation that occurs during periods of transition. It has been associated with rites of passage between one thing and another. Glynis Cousin likens this to adolescence, when we are not yet adults but not quite children: 'It is an unstable space in which the learner may oscillate between old and emergent understandings' 2006: 139). Whilst disorientation can be unsettling, it can also be seen as a threshold to something new, the fertile ground of creation: 'We are empty and receptive – erased tablets waiting for new words. Liminal space is where we are most teachable, often because we are most humbled. Liminality keeps us in an ongoing state of shadowboxing instead of ego-confirmation, struggling with the hidden side of things, and calling so-called normalcy into creative question' (Rohr, 2020 online). In the midst of a global crisis, we all face a state of liminality, as Rohr says we are caught between two worlds: 'Our consciousness and that of future generations has been changed. We cannot put the genie back in the bottle' (Ibid.).

Magical thinking

Our ability to be curious and to thrive in times of uncertainty is in itself a creative process. We have choices to make in our responses to events and in the ways in which we embrace or fight change. According to Gilbert (2015) the creative process is a form of disembodied energy – it is actually completely separate from us, but it is something we can interact with. Ideas are driven by an impulse of their own, by the desire to be known, but can only do this through human interaction As a result we may be 'visited' by ideas, and it is up to us to choose to work with them or not. In Gilbert's view, people often refuse their visitors, which then simply move on to the next candidate in order to be heard.

This idea may seem like magical thinking and not something for those who prefer a more scientific outlook, but we may also question whether there is a strict boundary between magic and science. The Alchemists of medieval times probably laid the foundation for modern-day chemistry, yet Alchemy would be considered somewhat magical. According to Koestler (1964) the separation between science and magic is not that clear. 'Unconscious, pre-rational, 'magical' thinking enters both into the creative act and into the beliefs or superstitions of the scientist. Quoting Dubos, he said, 'The alchemist never entirely ceased to live and function within the academician' (page 261).

Chapter reflections

In this chapter we have explored the meaning of creativity and the ways in which the creative process can be enhanced. The connections between reflective practice and encouraging creative thought have been discussed with reference to a range of practical strategies. Creativity, like reflection, is a personal thing and there is no 'one size fits all' approach, so it is important to try out a range of things, each of which might lead us somewhere interesting. Most important in all of this is maintaining a sense of curiosity as well as learning how to be comfortable in a liminal state. It is unlikely we will find all of the answers we seek by employing a single strategy and this is perhaps a benefit – if apparent answers are found immediately, we may well miss out on valuable insights that present themselves in the search.

References

Bandler, R. (2008) *Trans-formation, How to Harness the Power of Hypnosis to Ignite Effortless and Lasting Change*. Deerfield Beach, FL: HCI.

Bates, G. (1972) *Steps to an Ecology of Mind*. London: University of Chicago Press.

Calaprice, A. (2011) *The Ultimate Quotable Einstein*. Oxford: Princeton University Press.

Carroll, L. (1865) Available at: www.goodreads.com/work/quotes/17240250-through-the-looking-glassand-what-alice-found-there [date accessed 20/12/20].

Cousin, G. (2006) 'Threshold Concepts, Troublesome Knowledge and Emotional Capital: An Exploraton into Learning About Others'. In J. H. F. Meyer & R. Land (eds.), *Overcoming Barriers to Student Understanding: Threshold Concepts and Troublesome Knowledge*. London: Routledge, pp. 134–147.

Csikszentmihalyi, M. (1996) *Creativity: Flow and the Psychology of Discovery and Invention*. New York, NY: Harper Perennial.

Csikszentmihalyi, M. (2008) *Flow the Psychology of Optimal Experience*. New York, NY: Harper Perennial Modern Classics.

Einstein, A., & Infeld, L. (1967) *The Evolution of Physics, from Early Concepts to Relativity and Quanta*. New York, NY: Simon and Schuster. Reprint of original (1938).

Gilbert, E. (2015) *Big Magic, Creative Living Beyond Fear*. London: Bloomsbury.

Hall, E., & Leech, A. (1990) *Fantasy in the Classroom*. London. Routledge.

Koestler, A. (1964) *The Act of Creation*. London: Hutchinson and Co.

Murakami, H. (2014) *Men without Women*. London: Vintage.

Nielson, J. A., Zielinski, B. A., Ferguson, M. A., Lainhart, J. E., & Anderson, J. S. (2013) 'An Evaluation of the Left-Brain vs Right-Brain Hypothesis with Resting State Functional Connectivity Magnetic Resonance Imaging'. *PLoS One*, 8(8): e71275. doi: 10.1371/journal.pone.0071275.

Opezzo, M., & Schwartz, D. L. (2014) 'Give Your Ideas Some Legs: The Positive Effect of Walking on Creative Thinking'. *Journal of Experimental Psychology: Learning, Memory and Cognition*, 40(4): 1142–1152.

Picasso, P. (online) Available at: pablopicasso.org/quotes [date accessed: 24/12/20].

Robinson, K. (2017) *Out of our Minds, The Power of Being Creative* (3rd ed.). UK, Chichester: John Wiley and Sons Ltd.

Rogers, E. M. (2003) *Diffusion of Innovations* (5th ed.). New York, NY: Free Press.

Rohr, R. (2020) 'Between Two Worlds'. Available at: 1-liminalityrohr.pdf (wordpress.com) [date accessed: 23/12/20].

Rothenberg, A. (1971) 'The Process of Janusian Thinking in Creativity'. *Archives of General Psychiatry*, 24(3) (March 1): 195. doi: 10.1001/archpsyc.1971.01750090001001.

Samples, B. (1976) *The Metaphoric Mind: A Celebration of Creative Consciousness*. Boston, MA: Addison-Wesley Publishing Co.

Figure 8.1 Chapter mindmap

8 Joining up the dots

'What is the pattern that connects the crab to the lobster and the primrose to the orchid, and all of them to me, and me to you?' (Bateson, 1979: 8). Cybernetics' systems theory is focussed on developing an understanding of the interwoven nature of things, the idea that we are all parts of a system that is closely linked by a range of cause-and-effect relationships. According to Bateson, it is important to discover the pattern that connects by exploring how elements communicate and how human activity is affected by its environment. So far, we have considered the benefits of reflective practice in objectively viewing and critically evaluating not only our practice but our beliefs about it. This is the foundation upon which we can build effective change and strengthen the things that already work well. A fundamental part of this is finding the patterns that can lead to new discoveries.

'Joining up the dots' is a way of finding the patterns that have influence as well as the 'bit' of information which represents 'a difference that makes a difference' (Bateson, 1972: 315). Systemic thinking can be applied to challenging situations by exploring the interaction-patterns which influence them. By locating patterns – things that repeat in a predictable manner – there is the potential to influence change. Without this, change may become something driven by a process that has no real purpose, in that change is implemented simply because we feel the need to make a change but we have not necessarily considered the impact this will have on our context. There are many examples of this in organisations driven by a continuous quality improvement approach which can, if not effectively managed, lead to a scenario of change for change's sake. We tweak this and that in refining what we do, perhaps inching forward at a safe pace, perhaps going round in circles. Without the location of patterns, and the critical evaluation of them, we may also implement changes in the wrong areas and sometimes with devastating effects. I recall an 'old' student of mine who was struggling to manage the demands of work and life and, as a result began to question some of his choices. As he reminisced about the past, he explained that he had been divorced and remarried and told me that on reflection, he had realised there was nothing wrong with his first marriage but that he had felt the need for change. The problem was, he still felt the need for change. Sometimes we make assumptions when we should be seeking patterns!

DOI: 10.4324/9781003056812-9

Tom was a highly skilled professional working in a very specialised field. He liked his work but he also enjoyed his life outside of work, so he was not interested in gaining a promotion, he simply wanted to find a position that suited him and one in which he felt his expertise was appreciated. Unfortunately, this was proving to be more difficult than he had imagined. In the past 8 years he had changed jobs 4 times and he couldn't understand why it was so difficult to find something he liked. He always seemed to end up in the same situation – the work was fine, the team he worked with were OK . . . but for some reason he always ended up working with ambitious male bosses that he didn't like. Not a single one of them seemed able to communicate effectively, and he felt as if they were always talking at odds. After reflecting on his situation Tom decided that this issue was caused by the men working in his industry and that the only way he would find a job he liked would be to work with a female manager.

Tom's story isn't that unusual; he was unsettled at work and was looking for reasons why this might be the case. Our anxieties about work are often linked to our relationships with others, and Tom has certainly detected a pattern in that it is his relationship with his boss that is problematic. This seems to be something that repeats in a predictable way and Tom's reflection illustrates his assumptions about why this is the case. But what is missing from this reflection? Has Tom reflected on his own interaction patterns? Has he considered the part he might be playing in the way the pattern unfolds? Is the 'bit' of information that makes the difference to do with Tom's bosses – different people in each of the jobs, or is it to do with another constant pattern not yet uncovered? Tom has actually tried to address this issue by moving jobs several times, so he does have some evidence that the pattern may be a little more complex than he had first thought. That's the thing with patterns, something obvious might initially jump out at us and we pounce on it, hoping to resolve an issue quickly, but in doing so there is also the danger of addressing the wrong thing. In Tom's story and in the anecdotal example shared earlier in the chapter, the change required was probably not a change of boss (or wife), there was another underlying pattern that had not yet been discovered. By constructing their own stories to justify their choices both Tom and my 'old' student had managed to close down any further investigation.

Feedback loops

Feedback is simply information that at a personal level we can either choose to pay attention to or to ignore. Feedback is also a part of a bigger system which can be applied to many aspects of life. Feedback loops occur in nature, in businesses and in human relations. When we interact with people, animals or objects we receive some feedback. A person's words or actions represent a form of feedback, a dog's friendly nudge or growl does the same, and this feedback usually has the impact of moderating our own behaviour. When someone smiles at us, we might start a conversation; if they look away, we are unlikely to persist; if we receive a nudge from a friendly dog, we are likely to respond with a stroke but might move away if we get a growl. Our actions in turn provide feedback to others involved in the interaction. A technical representation of this would simply be that outputs from a system are fed back as inputs, which in turn influence outputs.

The idea of a feedback loop seems simple enough, particularly if we view them as a cause-and-effect model. However, simple causal relationships are not always easy to find because all parts of the system are providing feedback which influences the overall interaction, so A influences B and the response from B influences A . . . and so on. The only way to utilise this information is to look at the system as a whole – simply interpreting and adapting one single aspect of a system is unlikely to bring about the desired result.

There is a pre-supposition from neuro-linguistic programming (NLP) which illustrates this in terms of human communication: 'The meaning of your communication is the response you get.' A simple interpretation of this is that if you don't get the outcome you want from a specific interaction then you need to reflect on your part in that interaction, i.e., consider how your communication may have influenced things and adjust whatever aspect of that you deem to be lacking. At one level this is a very sensible assumption and if we all took this onboard we may well see a revelation in how we interact. The overall intent in the pre-supposition is sound – we should all consider and take responsibility for the way in which we communicate. However, it doesn't offer a complete picture. We could adjust our words and our style of communication to provide opportunity for the intended message to be received, but this will have little or no effect if the person receiving the message has already framed it in their own understanding and effectively hears something which reinforces their current understanding.

Tom's story is an example of this. Tom is involved in a feedback loop regarding his relationship with his male bosses. He has had the same experience several times, with several different people. Although Tom feels that the issue lies with his bosses – how likely is it that all of these people actually had the same character traits and the same ways of communicating? Tom was clearly receiving feedback which could have helped him change the way he was working with his managers, but he had a very definite frame around the system as a whole – in his view the men working in his industry all had personality traits he didn't admire. Based on this assumption, Tom had constructed a story about why his relationship with his bosses was problematic. He had also created an end to this tale, which was that the only way he would be happy at work would be if he were rescued by a female boss. Because of this, the likelihood is that whatever communication strategies Tom's bosses used, he would frame the interaction in the same way. In Chapter 4, we looked at types of distorted thinking which influence our understanding, and there are some of these evident in Tom's story. Some mental filtering is helping Tom to select the information he is paying attention to and there may well be some hidden 'should' statements within these interactions – Tom's bosses are not interacting with him in the way he thinks they should. In this case a simple adaptation in communication strategy is unlikely to have the desired result – or if it did, it would be quite short-lived.

Feedback loops provide information that results in repetition or avoidance of particular behaviours and if we are aware of them, we can adapt our behaviours accordingly to achieve the outcomes we want – simple! The trouble is, it isn't that simple as many responses to events happen at a level beyond our conscious awareness, so what we think are choices probably aren't choices at all; we may simply be reacting to events and when we don't get the outcomes we want, we are likely to look for forms of justification. As suggested in earlier chapters, we construct stories which offer acceptable explanations, providing a form of comfort blanket.

Constructing our stories

Booker (2004) discusses the importance of storytelling throughout history and highlights the similarities in these stories over the centuries by comparing the tale of *Beowulf* and *Jaws* – stories which are 1200 years apart, but which follow an almost identical plot. In analysing the structure of stories, he highlights the patterns which exist among them. For example, every story is likely to have a heroine or hero, maybe both. They are placed in an imaginary world; the general scene is set. We are introduced to the central characters and we know where the story will unfold. Then something will happen, an encounter which gives the story a focus, and this begins the series of adventures encapsulated in the tale. There will be some conflict, some uncertainty, probably a villain or two, but the protagonists will play their part in the adventures, which in some way will be transformational, until they reach the end. There are only two types of ending: one is happy, the other is not.

According to Booker, there are seven basic plots in all stories:

1   Overcoming the Monster – this is the story of a terrifying and powerful monster who is a threat to humankind. In this tale, the hero seeks out and, against all odds destroys the monster so that safety may be restored. The monster may be a dragon, a wicked witch, or perhaps a shark.

2   Rags to Riches – a young hero or heroine is living an ordinary life in difficult circumstances. One day an event sends them out into the world where they experience an adventure and eventually a magical transformation in their fortunes (and often themselves). Perhaps a bedraggled, Cockney flower-girl is picked up from the streets by a professor and is moulded into someone who can interact in fashionable society, an ugly duckling sets out into the world to become a beautiful swan, or a badly treated kitchen maid is helped to attend a ball where she meets and falls in love with a prince.

3   The Quest – this story begins with a call to action, a task which must be completed by the hero and his companions. This will usually involve a journey and a specific task such as casting a ring into a volcano, seeking treasure on an island, or finding a holy grail. The quest team will take a journey which subjects them to a number of ordeals and may have to overcome temptation and monsters along the way. Eventually, after completing mission impossible, they will achieve their goal with life-transforming impact.

4   Voyage and Return – this is the story in which the hero or heroine travel out of their familiar lives into another world. They don't necessarily have a purpose as in the Quest, so the nature of the story is more explorative. The new world starts out as exciting, if strange. Perhaps they travel through a wardrobe to the land of Narnia, or along a yellow brick road in the land of Oz. Gradually the mood changes as a shadow begins to pose a serious threat and the only desire left is to escape the new world and return home. A significant question at this point is whether anything was gained from the journey; were the characters transformed in any way or was this simply a dream?

5   Comedy presents us with a situation in which there is confusion or uncertainty which escalates into something of a tangle. Finally, there is a change in perception and the

story culminates in a happy ending. Comedy may well reflect the misunderstandings of life and love (as in many of Jane Austen's novels) but ultimately end in recognition of the mistakes made so that everyone can live happily ever after.

6   Tragedy – in this story we still have our hero or heroine who form part of a community through friendship, family or love – at some point the lead character will distance them-selves from these characters, will get caught up on a course of action that eventually leads to a violent or unnatural death. The story may include some rebellion or discov-ery and we may desperately want the characters to survive; we hope that Thelma and Louise will turn around and not drive off the cliff, or that Romeo realises Juliet is not dead but in a deep sleep . . . but as the story comes to a close, it becomes clear there is only one possible outcome.

7   Rebirth – the protagonist becomes overshadowed by a dark power which may grow and wane but eventually reveals its full force. It seems as if the dark power has triumphed and then there comes a redemption. In a Christmas Carol, Ebenezer Scrooge is haunted by the ghosts of Christmas past but, realising this is a dream, has a chance to redeem himself and be reborn.

Why are these stories important to us? When you think about it, our life is one long story and, as suggested in Chapter 1, metaphor plays an important role in how we make sense of life's twists and turns: 'We do not "store" experience as data, like a computer: we "story" it' (Winter, 1988: 235). How we construct our stories is key to our interpretation of them and performs a key role in reflection.

10-Minute Reflection – Once Upon a Time

Take a look at the seven basic plots again and select the one you are most drawn to. Then, using the basic tenets of the plot, construct a personal story. What patterns do you recognise? What does this tell you about how you are constructing your own story?

The purpose of this activity is to help locate patterns within our own stories. By plotting life's events in this way, we may also locate aspects of connection, pertinent twists in the tale and crossroads which led to important decisions.

Story telling is about more than the plot. A plot is simply a framework which gives an overall structure and as we can see from the examples provided here, stories can take many twists and turns before they lead to the ultimate outcome. They may even be a circuitous route to the starting point as in the voyage and return, but what are the characteristics of a *good* story? Very often, this centres around the characters – for me this is certainly true. If I don't like the lead characters in a book, I struggle to finish it, and when I watch a film, I can usually tell within ten minutes if I will enjoy it. Mostly this has to do with whether or not I can identify with the characters and more specifically, whether or not they appear to be authentic.

The authentic self

Authenticity is quite a tricky thing to define . . . in one way being ourselves is actually ines-capable: whatever we do or think, it is oneself who is doing that. However, we might also be inclined to say and do things because of external influences, perhaps because we think we should or because it is an expectation of a social or professional role. These things are not genuinely expressive of who we are and can challenge us at a visceral level. Not only is authenticity difficult to define, it may also be difficult to achieve because of the many expectations upon us and the behavioural patterns we have built up over a period of time. Even children soon learn what is expected of them and adapt their behaviours according to these expectations. As adults the situation is further complicated by our need to appear to be genuine so that others will trust us and want to interact with us.

The choices we make

Transendence is a term Sartre (2007) used to describe the human capability for being open to a range of possibilities to define themselves. Because humans are capable of reflection, they can actually put themselves into question and can distance sufficiently from the 'self' to question who they are and who they want to be. The notion is closely linked to the idea of freedom in that as humans we are free to choose how we interpret things and to decide what it is that matters or doesn't. We build our world through this freedom and at the same time create ourselves through our choices. This seems quite Utopian, having a range of choices and making our selection based on who we choose to be - it is a little like going into a shop and selecting a 'self' from the shelves, but as in most shops, choices can be limited and there is usually a price to pay for getting what we want. This of course is weighed up in the process of making our selection. Such decisions can be quite a responsibility, and we are well aware that there will be consequences if we get it wrong. This in turn may lead to what Sartre calls 'bad faith', whereby we stick to what is safe or familiar, thereby eliminat-ing other options and ultimately becoming victims of circumstance. Whilst we may pretend to ourselves that we do not have freedom to make choices, we are effectively *choosing* not to make a choice. This has the benefit of denying responsibility. For example, we might tell ourselves we cannot take a certain path because of external circumstances, such as family or work commitments and instead we can blame a situation or another person. We thereby spare ourselves from taking responsibility for our choices and, as a result, can lead an inauthentic life - which may well be more miserable than the outcome of any choices we might have made.

To do this, we have to construct a story around our choices which justifies them to our-selves and to others. Table 8.1 outlines some simple examples of this, providing a dilemma accompanied by the stories we might tell ourselves about the situation and some potential underlying reasons for not making a choice.

The examples provided are quite typical, but of course there is no formula involved in all of this. The stories we create are ones which are a good fit for what we believe, at least at a conscious level. We could even argue that our beliefs are inherently delusional. In truth, we rarely have full information as most of our information is based on perception, so we are

Table 8.1 Dilemmas and stories

Dilemma	Story	Underlying Concerns
Rebecca regularly says that she wants to lose weight, but this is proving very difficult.	Rebecca tells herself that healthy foods are expensive and exercise is costly. She can't afford to change her shopping habits or pay for a gym subscription.	Losing weight requires drastic changes to lifestyle – what if I fail?
Patrick is frustrated with his job. He finds it dull and feels he cannot use his talents.	Patrick has looked at opportunities in his field and there are very few jobs he could apply for. He tells himself he may as well 'grin and bear it'.	The job market is competitive – what if I am rejected?
Carolyn is unhappy in her marriage of 25 years. She wants to make a new life on her own but after all this time doesn't know where to start.	Carolyn decides that divorce will be too costly and would leave her in financial difficulty. She tells herself she can take pleasure in her hobbies and her friends.	Being single means you only have yourself to rely on – what if I can't cope on my own?
Jeff has been working in a dead-end job for years. Now in his 40s, he realised that he had always wanted to be a teacher but he had no qualifications.	Jeff tells himself that he is too old to retrain. He may as well make the most of what he has and look forward to retirement.	Retraining is a big step and could be a long journey – what if I find studying too difficult, or I can't get a job when I graduate?

often filling in the missing blanks with whatever seems acceptable at the time . . . and that brings us back to our stories.

Making informed choices

Recognising the connections between aspects of experience helps us to determine the impact of our choices and helps to raise our awareness of whether or not something is a good fit for us. When we have awareness that one change will influence another, as identified in the feedback loop, we are more likely to implement changes that will have the best overall outcome. At the same time, it helps us to recognise that there are no perfect solutions; the choices we make will all have an impact on a part of the system, but by anticipating this we can recognise the trade-offs and make more informed choices.

10-Minute Reflection – 5 Steps

1   Outline a problem, concern or event that you have been thinking about.
2   List as many aspects of it as you can. Write down anything you have any information about and list each thing separately.
3   Go back over the list and highlight any connections between the various parts.
4   Then look for common themes or repeating patterns.
5   Finally, rewrite the event or concern.

The purpose of this activity is to search out connections and patterns which may ultimately help us to redefine a concern. This is based on the premise that our initial reflection (in point 1) may well be based on a story we are telling ourselves, and the rewrite in point 5 has the benefit of having outlined connections and patterns. The outlines in points 1 and 5 may well end up being the same, which simply means that the initial concern was objectively recorded.

As a child, Serena was told she should not expect too much out of life. Life was hard and it was only the people advantaged at birth who were given the opportunities to make something of themselves. It was best, her mother told her, if she kept her head down, kept herself safe and was thankful for what she had – after all, she didn't have any talents and wasn't especially pretty. The 'advantages at birth' floating around the maternity ward had not settled on her! Serena did her mother's bidding and played safe. She never put herself forward for anything, she simply settled for what was offered. This rule applied to her career and her personal relationships, and whilst she couldn't exactly say she was happy, her life wasn't awful. She had learned to be thankful for what she had. One thing she was thankful for was her walks – they were her greatest pleasure. She would amble through the woods, along the river and through open fields, breathing in the sights and sounds of nature and enjoying her solitude. She walked the same routes so often she knew every inch of each path. One day, when Serena was walking through the woods, she noticed the bright sunlight peeking through the trees. It seemed to cast a magical light like diamonds sparkling amongst the lush green. More than that, it shone a light on her and led her on a different route, where she noticed things she hadn't seen before.

Although her pragmatic head told her that she probably hadn't undergone a transformation, Serena felt different. She had noticed so many new things, the patterns on foliage, the way the tree roots were entangled with brambles, the interconnecting patterns of nature. Like the patterns of life. The event in the woods seemed to have awakened her, dissolving the heavy weight of her childhood beliefs. Those beliefs were no longer truths, they were simply patterns – her mother's patterns playing out in her own life.

Serena hadn't discovered any new talents on that walk or transformed from an ugly duckling into a beautiful swan, but she had started to think about her life rather than amble through it, and in doing so, she had made the decision that it was time to make some changes.

Changing patterns

Given some of the difficulties outlined in this chapter it would be easy to assume that change might be out of our control. In some respects this is true – there are aspects of change that we cannot influence, but there are others that we can. We may not control external events, but with awareness we can manage our reactions to them. Butler *et al.* (2018) outline three steps to implementing change:

- Understand the present
- Step lightly from the past
- Accept the uncertainty of the future

Understanding the present

Understanding the present is at the heart of reflective practice. The point of questioning and critically evaluating events is that we gain an objective and deeper understanding of them. In effect the art of reflection is about stepping away from habits of thinking so that we have a less biased view of events within our current environment. This is essential as we can only make choices about future actions from our present. It is important that we don't hide current reality by constructing stories around it but that we simply accept it in the knowledge that if there are aspects of the present that we do not like, we can plan to change them, not by a process of wishful thinking by a process of thoughtful action. Serena's story outlines an event that seemed to awaken her thinking and give her a more detailed understanding of the present. The reference to 'ambling through life' suggested habits of thinking that had kept her safe but also less than happy. In a sense her tale is a rags-to-riches story; by opening her mind to new ways of thinking she has the potential to make different choices, leading to different paths and maybe to buried treasure! Conversely, Tom seemed to be caught up in a comedy. His relationships with various bosses are consistently influenced by misinterpretations and confused messages. For this story to have a happy ending there would need to be a change of perception and recognition of mistakes made.

Stepping lightly from the past

In Serena's story we see someone who, at a young age, had been taught not to expect too much out of life and to be grateful for her lot. This message, so inculcated into her life, had become her story. She would play safe, keep her head down and if she continued to do this, her story would also continue in much the same way as it had before. Similarly, Tom's story is a repeating pattern of blaming others for problems in communication, which without honest reflection and a more critical evaluation of events will simply continue to play out much as it has to date.

When viewed objectively and without emotion, past events simply represent feedback. If we review the stories we have constructed around them and step lightly away, they also present an opportunity to analyse what we would like to change. After this, we are able to define and then implement steps to move towards the desired change. Past events most certainly have an impact on how we think and feel, but they don't have to define us. Was it Jung who said 'I am not what happened to me, I am what I choose to become'?

Accepting the uncertainty of the future

There are no guarantees that when we choose to make changes, we will also choose the right path or the right strategy to implement them. As we can't foresee what will happen in the future, we must also accept that there is likely to be some uncertainty in relation to the outcomes. That can be challenging but is made far less challenging when we develop an attitude of openness to whatever change brings alongside the confidence to know that we are able to cope with whatever outcomes are presented.

Chapter reflections

In this chapter we have examined the interconnectedness of experience. By recognising the ways in which different parts of a system influence each other, we are able to view reflection in a more holistic way. Reflection, when purely driven by a focus on finding a solution, might lead us to alter an aspect of what we do based on a single event or piece of information; but if this doesn't take into account the connections to other aspects of practice, we may well change the wrong thing. We may simply be skirting around the issue without getting to the most important aspect of it: 'We dance around in a ring and suppose; But the Secret sits in the middle – and knows' (Frost in Booker, 2004). Ultimately, effective change is based on finding the difference that will make a difference, and as our practice takes place in a context, we must also take into account what surrounds it.

References

Bateson, G. (1972) *Steps to an Ecology of Mind*. London: University of Chicago Press.

Bateson, G. (1979) *Mind and Nature, a Necessary Unit*. New York, NY: E. P. Dutton.

Booker, C. (2004) *The Seven Basic Plots, Why We Tell Stories*. London: Bloomsbury.

Butler, G., Grey, N., & Hope, T. (2018) *Managing Your Mind – The Mental Fitness Guide* (3rd ed.). Oxford: Oxford University Press.

Sartre, J-P. (2007) *Existentialism is a Humanism*. New Haven: Yale University Press.

Winter, R. (1988) 'Fictional-Critical Writing'. In J. Nias & S. Groundwater-Smith (eds.), *The Enquiring Teacher*. London: Falmer, pp. 231-248.

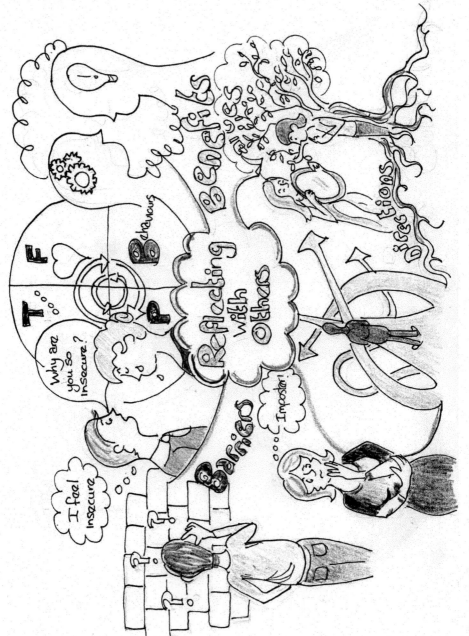

Figure 9.1 Chapter mindmap

9 Reflecting with others

The importance of continued development shouldn't be underestimated. It shouldn't be seen as an aspiration but a key ingredient of professionalism as without it we are unlikely to grow to our full potential. Organisations and professions learn as individuals learn, and very often, individuals learn by interacting with others. In Chapter 2, we looked at the ways in which we learn in context, through our experience in the workplace and through communities of practice. In this chapter we will review the benefits of reflecting with others and the strategies we might use to make the most of this opportunity.

The benefits of reflecting with others

Learning with others is a natural part of human development in whatever form it takes. We may benefit from Incidental learning which takes place through our experiences and our relationships, or learning could be more structured and be directed by others. Social learning theory is based on the premise that interaction is a fundamental part of how we learn (Bandura, 1986). We do this by observing the actions and interactions of others, which is not dissimilar to the way that other species learn. Young animals often mimic the behaviours of the adults in their groups and in a similar way, children are very prone to copying the ways in which the significant adults in their lives behave. The danger here of course is that we also learn to copy behaviours that are not necessarily desirable. In terms of reflecting with others this may be something of a drawback, and for this reason it is important to consider some of the issues related to reflecting in groups as well as recognising the benefits.

As suggested in earlier chapters, there are clear benefits to committing our reflections to paper and in doing so we are giving them some status. Once translated into words or images, thoughts become real in the sense that we have to acknowledge them. The same can be said for verbally expressing reflections when we share them with others. One important benefit to this practice is that other people are likely to bring different perspectives. In Chapter 3, we looked at the lenses model (Brookfield, 2017) which is built on the premise of gaining a range of perspectives to inform our reflections. In this model we are encouraged to view reflections through the perspectives of students, colleagues and theories as well as taking into account our own views. In addition to widening perspectives, other people are likely to

DOI: 10.4324/9781003056812-10

ask us questions about our reflections, which may help extend our thinking. Reflecting with others may help to:

- Clarify strengths and areas for development
- Improve our decision making
- Enhance awareness of the beliefs and values that guide our actions
- Improve relationships with colleagues
- Save time

Although solitary reflection will enhance awareness of strengths and areas for development, it has the limitation of just offering one perspective, and depending on our self-efficacy, this is highly likely to be weighted more heavily on one side than the other. We may be very good at seeing our weaknesses and less good at seeing our strengths or vice versa. Having the benefit of alternative perspectives is also helpful in decision-making as this provides more information for consideration as well as the shared experiences of others who have most likely had to make the same decisions at one point.

Whilst, I would certainly advocate gaining a clear understanding of the values and beliefs that underpin our practice, I am also aware that this is not as easy as it seems. In chapter three this was illustrated by the concept of espoused theories and theories in use: the difference between the values we believe our behaviour is based on (and the ones we are likely to articulate) as opposed to the values implied by our behaviours (Argyris & Schön, 1974). For example, someone may espouse the idea of speaking up against authority figures but be very silent when the opportunity presents itself.

Values represent things that are important to us – they tell us what matters and can be viewed as our life directions. As they are directions, rather than goals, they are likely to be something that is never reached. Instead they provide a way of being. Although values are important in providing life direction, not all of them are obvious and some take on the form of underground activists in that they direct our thoughts and behaviours but can be hidden. For this reason, checking-in with our values from time to time is a useful activity.

10-Minute Reflection – Value Checker

Think about a positive event that was meaningful for you. How did you feel? What values were being met by this event? Write down as many as come to mind. Now, flip this around to a time when you felt angry, frustrated or upset. How did you feel? What values were being suppressed by this event?

The purpose of this activity is to highlight the core values brought to mind by reflecting on an emotional response to particular events. It is possible that you may have a big list, in which case try grouping them until you can whittle the list down a little. You will know which the core values are as you will be unable to take those out of your list. Talking to others may also help. When we do this, we not only share our values by articulating them but also have the opportunity to explore them further by listening to others' understandings and by asking and answering questions. This is also a good strategy for building collegiality. There is nothing more reassuring than realising that we share values with our colleagues and that we very often share the same frustrations. Reflecting together not only allows these things to be aired, it provides a supportive forum in which we might discuss concerns.

Reflection is a powerful tool for enhancing understanding and for developing our practice, but it can also be time-consuming, especially when we get stuck chasing a particular train of thought down a rabbit hole! Sometimes it can be difficult to pinpoint the key aspects of an issue and we end up going round and round in circles. When we reflect with others, we are required to verbalise our thoughts and, in doing so, have to select the most pertinent points and put them in a logical order. This action alone may help to clarify some reflections and a further benefit is that other's questions may help to elicit insights.

Potential barriers

Whilst there are clearly many benefits to reflecting with others, it is also useful to consider some of the barriers. When a reflection group extends beyond 2 people, the relationship becomes more complex. Beneath surface behaviours lie the beliefs and values of several people, and above the surface these are presented in a range of ways. For some, trust and intimacy within a group setting are considered quite risky, and if the dynamic isn't managed effectively this may result in a range of defensive behaviours, such as:

- Concern with the image we are presenting to the group
- Trying to dominate the discussion
- Being judgemental
- Avoiding the expression of authentic feelings

There is also the danger of groupthink (as outlined in Chapter 6), whereby, in an attempt to fit in with the group we may superficially adopt values and ideas and avoid conflict by conforming to the dominant ideology within the group.

Valuing ourselves in the group process

We can all be guilty of undervaluing ourselves and our achievements. For example, when I completed the value checker reflection in this chapter, I was reminded of the viva examination required for my doctorate, something which I approached with significant anxiety. There is a certain amount of fear surrounding this process not helped by colleagues recounting vignettes of challenging examiners whose apparent aim was to tear apart the work they had spent years on! My expectations of the event were not positive but my experience of it was. I suppose I had gone into it expecting to be challenged . . . after all, who was I to think I could produce work that would meeting such exacting requirements? But I came out of it feeling pleasantly surprised and pleased about my achievement, especially by the idea that I had produced something of value. An objective view of this event would have taken into consideration the amount of work that had gone into the research and would have acknowledged the experience underlying it – but all I could think of was that it might not be good enough and that I would do or say something that would lead to a failure. This reminded me of two values: one which is openly acknowledged – the importance of creating work of use to others. The other lurks hiding in the murky depths. and that is that what I do might not be quite 'good enough'.

Imposter syndrome

That sense of not being quite good enough is quite common, particularly in professional roles and often among people who are well qualified. It is based on the fear that we will be discovered as a fraud when other people discover the truth that we don't have all the answers (Clance & Imes, 1978). Left unchecked this can become a barrier in professional practice, and when reflecting with others creates a hurdle as it presents in a lack of confidence to share expertise.

Seeing one's own sense of value can be difficult for a number of reasons. If we feel we are expected to have all the answers or are encouraged to be modest or not to 'show off' this can so easily inform our behaviour and become habitual. We may even develop double standards, in that we find it quite easy to recognise and value positive qualities in others but not in ourselves. In group scenarios this can lead to limiting behaviours which don't serve us or the group as a whole.

Elena dreaded going to team meetings, which felt a little like entering a gladiator's ring. Within her team there were 2 or 3 people who tended to dominate discussion, challenging each other until there was a victory. It seemed like nothing much was achieved other than individuals winning or losing a battle. The discussions seemed to go down paths that led them to the same place, no further forward than when the meeting began. She often wanted to intervene but knew that it was pointless. She wasn't a 'key player', so no-one was interested in what she had to say. She even had proof of this as on the one occasion she had tried to contribute to the discussion, her comments had been completely ignored. This was not only upsetting, it also made her question herself. She had always believed it was important to stand up for her convictions and yet she had simply allowed others to ignore her contribution.

There are three common reasons why we undervalue ourselves (Butler *et al.*, 2018):

- A sense of not being 'good enough'
- Thinking we appear arrogant
- Believing we have been 'bad'

Each of these factors will influence how we interact with others. In Elena's story we see someone who views herself as not being important, not a key player, therefore not 'good enough' to take part in the team discussions. When she did try to contribute this was ignored, reinforcing her perception that she wasn't seen as a 'key player' and that others would not be interested in what she had to say.

The opposite scenario is when we come across as valuing our own opinions more than others, which may appear arrogant and at the very least is unfair to others within the group. It seems that the 'gladiators' in Elena's team suffered from a sense of self-importance, which meant that they dominated discussions and didn't pay any attention to what others had to say. However, by undervaluing herself Elena is actually doing the same thing but in reverse; she is not being fair to herself because she is not putting forward her views, and it could be argued she is actually devaluing the work of the team by not offering an alternative perspective.

It is also possible to undervalue ourselves because we are disappointed in ourselves because we haven't come up to our own personal standards in terms of behaviour. Elena had always believed that it was important to stand by your convictions, but she hadn't been able to do this in the team meetings and this was disappointing.

People are complex and have many sides to their personalities. Although Elena's story presents a tale of difficult characters who seem to be leading the team down well-trodden and ineffective paths, it is unlikely that this is all there is to that story. There are social pressures within any workplace which influence how individuals behave. We also have echoes from the past which determine how we interact and may lead to defensive behaviours that are not necessarily helpful in a group setting.

Power and personal processes

When groups are set up, someone takes responsibility for managing the process, whether it be as group leader or facilitator. Whatever way that person positions themselves in this scenario, there is still some power within the role and other members of the group will recognise this and expect the leader to offer some guidance so that things run smoothly. Authority in the role of group leader is variable depending on the group and the context, so it is useful to be open about it from the outset. By acknowledging that some authority and responsibility are attached to the role, we may discuss potential boundaries and structure the group in a way that suits its purpose.

> Eric was keen to set up a research and reading group amongst his colleagues as he felt this would be a useful forum for professional development. He had been really excited about the idea and was keen to get started, but now, after three meetings he was feeling less than enthusiastic. There were only 6 members in the group, but he felt that the meetings were dominated by one person, Janetta, a rather assertive character who was very open to sharing her opinions. Janetta wasn't someone Eric had worked with before, nor did he know anything about her, but for some reason she seemed strangely familiar. What Eric found quite disconcerting about this was that his response to Janetta seemed to be quite automatic; he didn't really think through what he said to her and was often defensive, sometimes even aggressive. This left him feeling embarrassed that he had shown this side of his character to his colleagues, and what had started out as an adventure had now become something he dreaded.

All groups are different and take on a life of their own but there are several dynamics that are common and worth consideration:

Transference and counter-transference – these are terms often used in therapeutic relationships, but they aren't just reserved for therapy, they happen in any human interaction. Transference is where we might associate a person with a past or present relationship. It is a redirection of feelings towards them. For example, the group leader may be seen by the member of the group as a parent figure and feelings towards that parent (positive or negative) will be associated with the new relationship. This is a subconscious process – sometimes people might seem familiar but we don't understand why. Counter-transference is what happens in the opposite direction. In Eric's case this was the unexpected (and unwanted) reactions he had to Janetta, made even more frustrating because he couldn't understand why he was reacting in the way that he was. Even for people skilled in human relations it isn't easy to recognise transference. The best approach is to acknowledge when something feels a little 'off' and make a note of your own responses so that you can alter them if required.

Projection – the ways in which we have learned to interpret our experiences helps us to make judgements on a range of things, including other people. Throughout life we learn things about ourselves, some of which we openly accept and others which we may deny or not be fully aware of. The act of projecting takes the form of blame shifting. We deny the existence of aspects of ourselves by attributing them to other people, as Matè suggests: 'When I am sharply judgemental of any other person, it's because I sense or see reflected in them some aspect of myself that I don't want to acknowledge' (2009: 254). It is possible that Eric, disappointed with the way he is leading the group, may also be projecting some of his feelings onto Janetta.

Introjection – is another defense mechanism and is the opposite of projection. In this case we unconsciously adopt the attitudes and ideas of others. For example, children may introject their parents' ideas of right and wrong. This also happens in the workplace when people unthinkingly adopt the beliefs of a team or organisation. Introjections are usually adopted from influential people in our lives. They aren't really digested or analysed they are simply swallowed whole.

Connectedness

In Chapter 8 we discussed ideas of connectedness within systems, using the theory of feedback loops to explain how one system interacts with another. A group is another form of system, so the same applies in this scenario. As we have seen from the case studies, the actions of one person in a group may cause different reactions in another and these can be both positive and negative. Relationships are complex!

The 5-part model outlines the ways in which this works on a personal level by considering how thoughts influence feelings, behaviours and physical reactions and all of these happen within a given context (Padesky, 2020). The model depicts how each of the four aspects interrelate and a change in one can influence change in another.

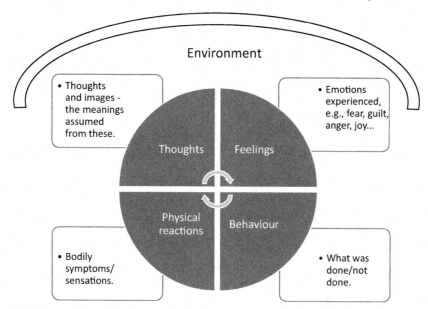

Figure 9.2 Five-part model
Source: Adapted from Padesky, 2020

Ways of reflecting with others

Although I have outlined a number of drawbacks in reflecting with others, this has only been done to raise awareness of potential issues. There are still many benefits to the process if we accept that it is perfectly imperfect. In acknowledging this, we are more prepared to embrace the imperfections.

There are a number of ways that we can structure opportunities for reflecting with others including:

Setting up a mentoring or buddying system – this provides an opportunity to develop relationships between individuals, usually over the longer term. It might be used to support a course of study or a period of transition.

Reading groups – provide an opportunity for people to set aside time to interact with literature relevant to their area and discuss any changes in thinking or implications for practice.

Peer observations – a useful source of inspiration and reflection. By observing others' practice, we have the opportunity to explore different approaches and reflect on what may be incorporated into or adapted for our own work.

Support groups – offer a forum to reflect on specific aspects of practice. They provide a safe environment in which to discuss the more difficult aspects of work, enabling participants to develop deeper understanding of issues in a community of supportive peers.

Writing groups – although set up for the purpose of producing written artefacts, these can also provide scope for reflecting with others who may offer alternative perspectives on our ideas.

Enabling the process

When we reflect with others, we do so to enhance our own development as well as to co-construct new learning. This is about trying to be the best that we can be, what Rogers referred to as becoming a 'fully functioning person' (Rogers, 1961). In order to achieve this, it is important to develop a positive self-image based on genuineness, in which case we might display the following characteristics:

- Lack of defensiveness
- Openness to experience
- A flexible approach to others
- An ability to trust our own experiences and form values based on them
- A willingness to listen to feedback from others
- An ability to develop harmonious relationships

The group itself should be one in which members can feel accepted by others without being judged. Any communication will be enhanced if it is conducted in a framework which emphasises mutual respect. Rogers uses the term 'unconditional positive regard' to illustrate the humanistic principle that people are inherently good and seek personal growth and fulfilment, therefore we should respect individual choices and contributions to the group.

In addition, it is important that group members are able to show empathy and genuineness. This enhances the feelings of security that any views shared are being heard and understood by others and that others are sharing their own reflections with a sense of openness.

Setting up a reflection group

Reflective practice can be very personal to individuals and, if the aim is to set up a safe space in which to explore reflections, it is worth spending some time thinking about the best way of structuring the group. Taking into account that all groups are different and evolve in different ways, the following are simply offered as suggestions on the premise that groups also change and grow, so what works initially may need to be re-evaluated at a later date.

- Decide on the overall purpose and scope of the group. Is it going to be a forum for offering support? Is the aim to investigate developments in practice? Is it about professional development for its members? Will group members be expected to produce any outputs (as in a writing group)? What are the limitations of the group?
- Consider group membership. Is the group open to anyone or to people in particular roles? For membership to be beneficial does it require any background knowledge or expertise?
- Should there be ground rules or a contract for members? If so, how will these be established?
- Are there any ethical considerations – is there a particular code of ethics which needs to be followed?
- How will group meetings be run? Will there be a leader? If so, will leadership remain static or move between group members? If not, how will the group process be managed?

Creating a positive climate

Most groups whose focus is reflection need very little in the way of resources as the main resource is the group itself. The most important aspect of climate relates to social aspects, such as the creation of a safe space in which people feel they can openly share information and, as suggested earlier in the chapter, consideration should be given to how this can be achieved.

There may be some practical considerations, such as the space used for the activity. Many of the reading groups I have participated in have taken place in open spaces where people traffic is free-flowing, but this would not be appropriate for a support group where people may be sharing sensitive information. In addition to the space, consideration needs to give to what other resources may be required (such as chairs, tables or facilities for sharing information like whiteboards).

Facilitating the group process

Once the purpose and practice of the group have been established, attention can be turned to how best to facilitate the process of group reflection. The following points are relatively straight-forward to implement if there is a group leader or facilitator but require more detailed thought if there is not.

- Encourage members of the group to talk by asking prompting questions or by starting a discussion.
- Actively encourage support between participants by making connections, for example, 'Jeff made a good point about that last week . . .' or 'I think Anne has some experience of that. . . .'
- Use open-ended and probing questions. This is anything that avoids a yes/no answer and requires the respondent to provide some detail, such as: 'What was your experience of . . .?', 'How did that work in . . .?', 'In what ways was that . . .? The Socratic method outlined in Chapter 3 may be useful to provide some specific examples of how to probe rationale and assumptions.
- Offer verbal support if appropriate. If a group member is experiencing difficulty expressing their reflections, you may be able to help by sharing similar examples of your own whilst acknowledging that there will be obvious differences.
- Don't dominate the discussion – that seems obvious, but it would be remiss not to include it.
- Be sure to give everyone the chance to talk (but respect that they might choose not to).
- Remember that dynamics may change over time and the group may need to revisit its purpose and process.
- Try to start and finish on time. A 5-minute drift is not a big problem, but it is important to respect that people have other commitments.

Chapter reflections

In this chapter we have considered the benefits of reflecting in groups and highlighted some of the drawbacks. Particular attention has been given to individual experiences of group processes as this can be difficult for a lot of people and may discourage them from taking up opportunities to participate, and therefore is a key consideration for group leaders and participants.

References

Argyris, M., & Schön, D. (1974) *Theory in Practice. Increasing Professional Effectiveness.* San Francisco, CA: Jossey-Bass.

Bandura, A. (1986) 'The Explanatory and Predictive Scope of Self-Efficacy Theory'. *Journal of Clinical and Social Psychology,* 4(3): 359-373.

Brookfield, S. (2017) *Becoming a Critically Reflective Teacher.* San Francisco, CA: Jossey-Bass.

Butler, G., Grey, N., & Hope, T. (2018) *Managing Your Mind - The Mental Fitness Guide* (3rd ed.). Oxford: Oxford University Press.

Clance, P., & Imes, S. (1978) 'The Imposter Phenomenon in High Achieving Women: Dynamics and Therapeutic Intervention'. *Psychotherapy Theory, Research and Practice,* 15(3): 1-8.

Matè, G. (2009) *In the Realm of Hungry Ghosts, Close Encounters with Addiction.* Toronto: Vintage Canada.

Padesky, C. A. (2020) *The Clinician's Guide to CBT Using Mind Over Mood* (2nd ed.). New York, NY: The Guildford Press.

Rogers, C. R. (1961) *On Becoming a Person - A Therapist's View of Psychotherapy.* New York, NY: Haughton Mifflin Company.

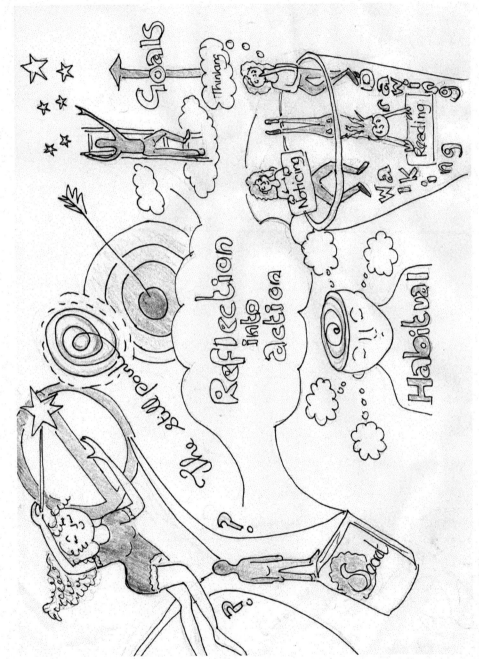

Figure 10.1 Chapter mindmap

10 Turning reflection into action

'I wish I was your age and knew what I know now.' This phrase sticks in my mind for a number of reasons. The first time I heard it I was around 16 years old and a somewhat shy teenager who didn't feel confident enough to question the wisdom of the elders who offered this gem. To me it seemed like such a profound statement. *What was this big secret? What was this one thing* (in my mind it was a single entity) *which I needed to learn in order to become wise? And when would I be old enough to learn it?* Well, the sad news is ... I still can't answer those questions! Furthermore, I suspect that the sages who offered these seemingly wise words couldn't answer them either. There is no 'secret', no magic wand, no single approach that will ensure your life is successful ... but you probably already know that. The reason I have included this anecdote is because to me it represents our constant search for knowledge, our need to not only understand the world around us but to understand ourselves. Maybe that's what the elders of my teenage years meant, maybe not.

One thing I probably do know now that I didn't know when I was 16, is how quickly life moves on and the importance of finding the still point in a turning world (Eliot, 1936). Eliot's poem 'Burnt Norton' portrays how present and past inform the future, suggesting that: 'If all time is eternally present ... All time is unredeemable.' Finding the still point for me, is finding the time to make sense of my work and my world: 'at the still point, there the dance is.' This is the essence of reflection.

How reflection develops practice

In chapter one we explored reasons for developing the habit of reflection to allow us to think deeply about our practice, and in later chapters we have explored other areas of reflection such as the role it plays in finding patterns and enhancing creativity. All of this is very useful, and learning the skills required to reflect openly and critically is something that all professionals should embrace. On that premise, I offer two bold statements:

- Reflective practice is not something that automatically happens – we need to make an effort to reflect critically.
- We do not get better at what we do simply by virtue of experience – contrary to popular belief, it isn't simply a case of becoming older and wiser. We actually have to know what we do well and less well and then locate ways of improving the things which could be better.

DOI: 10.4324/9781003056812-11

To refer to the previous anecdote, when my elders talked of the usefulness of their acquired knowledge, they were probably reflecting on the choices they had made, rather than a treasure trove of secret knowledge. The passing of time does afford us insights into where our choices lead. We learn how things turn out simply because we experience them. But who is to say where a different path would have taken us and whether it would have been preferable to the one we have taken? Different choices, missed opportunities. . . . It is purely speculation.

In my youth, 'I wish I knew then what I know now' signalled an exciting adventure ahead of me and one in which I would learn many things. Now the statement speaks of regrets . . . of choices made or not made and of paths well-trodden or never taken. It also tells me how important it is to reflect in this moment – to make this a part of the journey so that we may make better choices and hopefully have fewer regrets. With that in mind, I offer a third bold statement:

- Reflection only leads to change if we do something with it.

Reflection, even self-indulgent naval gazing, may well afford us some insights into thoughts, behaviours and choices and as a result we may develop greater self-awareness, but if we continue to do things in exactly the same way, to make the same choices and follow the same habitual paths, then its usefulness is limited. If change is desired, reflection must be accompanied by action.

> ### 10-Minute Reflection – Change Mindmap
>
> Using your preferred method of mindmapping reflect on the things you would like to change. Try to think of several areas where you might like to make changes and make each one of these a branch on your map. Then think about how you might go about making these changes. What strategies do you need to employ? What framework should be in place to support success? Add any ideas to the relevant branches. Mindmaps can be a creative process so the use of colour and images is helpful.

Mindmaps present a graphical organiser and allow you to get your ideas down as they occur to you. You can then add to them as new things occur to you. They are a great way of exploring new topics, generating ideas or simply organising your thoughts and have the benefit of being able to accommodate a lot of information on a single sheet. However, to be useful they do need to be approached with a sense of openness and possibility. This ensures that mental barriers are not set up from the outset.

> Marielle loved planning new projects – both in her professional life and her personal life. She always had something new to focus on and loved the stage of putting together her ideas in the form of a mindmap or a mood board. Some of her friends thought this approach was a little fluffy, but Marielle knew that she was very pragmatic in her approach. She always thought about the practicalities of achieving her aims, and she always managed to do whatever she set out to do. This should have been reward in itself, but Marielle felt that there was something missing. Whilst she set out aims and achievement strategies with complete ease, she never actually felt like she was getting what she wanted.

Strategies such as mindmaps and mood boards (a mood board is created out of images and tactile objects meant to evoke emotions around a particular topic) are useful tools in putting together ideas and can prove to be a creative and sometimes therapeutic process. However, they will not move forward thinking if they are too limited by practical considerations. In Marielle's case, whilst she was using a creative approach to records her dreams, she was also limiting them from the outset by focussing too much on practicalities, and this may have been creating a block to recording what she really wanted to believe. By being overly pragmatic, she was limited in the things she allowed herself to hope for and as a result, even after achieving the things she set out to achieve, she still felt a sense of disappointment. This isn't to suggest that practical considerations should be ignored. They are actually a very important part of goal creation, but they need to be considered at the right point in the process – making them a focus too early simply limits idea generation.

5-Minute Reflection - No Limits

Write down your ideas in relation to the following statement:
'If there were absolutely no limits, what would I choose to do?'
It is important to allow free thought without imposing any limits. The focus is on what you want to do, not what you can or should do.

Habitual ways of thinking and doing do provide a sense of security, but they also impose limits. When we try to generate ideas within the framework of what we normally think and do then we are automatically limiting our options for development. The 'no limits' reflection provides the scope to look beyond what is current and has a focus on extending our thinking to allow the generation of new ideas.

Choose your own path

As discussed in previous chapters, the process of reflection is individual. There are many models which may offer structure and a number of tools which can provide a kick-start or a motivational boost when required. All of the 5-and 10-minute strategies used in this book can be used in this way, and for ease they have been combined in one of the appendices.

It is unlikely that there will be a single activity which meets all reflection needs; your own individual process may be made up of many elements. To illustrate this, I have offered an overview of the things that work for me. It was difficult to present this in any sort of order and whilst a nice, linear flow chart might have been easier to follow, it wouldn't really represent how I experience the process. The elements that make up my own reflective practice are illustrated by the key words in Figure 10.2 and include:

- Noticing the detail of events and my reactions to them
- Writing down what happened alongside thoughts and feelings
- Drawing to generate ideas or to gain clarity

- Reading to explore interesting topics further and widen perspectives
- Walking to occupy my body with an easy activity whilst my mind is allowed to wander
- Thinking, which often involves putting together the various parts as well as accepting where the parts simply don't fit

I believe all of these things help to bring about new perspectives and offer more choices. In addition, it helps to develop my understanding of what I do and how I do it, acceptance of the things I can't change as well as the generation of ideas for the things that I can. It is a melting pot of activity with no definite beginning or end.

This is a book about reflection, so it is fair to say that the landscape of reflective practice has been painted in a positive light, and it is hoped that the content of preceding chapters has helped in forming your own approach to the process. We have discussed the wide-reaching

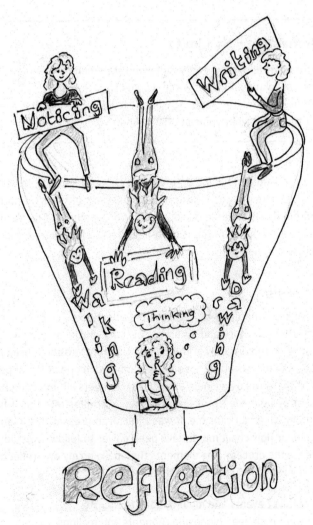

Figure 10.2 Sample reflection process

potential of adopting a reflective approach, but it is acknowledged that it isn't a panacea and as previously stated will only be useful if we do something with it. This means that there are two steps to take. The first is to find out what works for you in terms of a reflective process, and some of the tools outlined in Chapter 6 may help with this. The second is to think about how you can turn reflection into action, which will involve thinking about aspects of change.

5-Minute Reflection – stream of consciousness writing

Briefly think about the things that may work for you in the reflective process. Then set a timer for five minutes and write uninterrupted. Write whatever comes to mind and ignore normal conventions such as punctuation and spelling. It doesn't matter if the words or thoughts lack coherence, and they are likely to do this quite naturally.

Stream of consciousness writing is often used in literature to portray an individual's point of view. The key idea is that the writing occurs in a flow and is not disturbed by any form of editing. It can also be used as a therapeutic tool as it is completely uncensored. We all have disconnected thoughts and feelings that often go unacknowledged because we can't make sense of them. This strategy allows them to be recorded, and they may be reviewed at a later date when things do begin to make more sense.

Goals and targets

The words 'goal' and 'target' are often used interchangeably, but of course they are not the same thing. When we talk about goals, we are referring to primary ambitions such as setting up a small business, writing a book or creating a community project. These are the overall things we want to achieve, and most people will only work on one or two goals at a time. Targets are specific aims. They are a marking point on the journey, and it is through the achievement of targets that we achieve our overall goals.

Alejandro had really enjoyed the first six months of his new role but was a little apprehensive about his performance development review. In his last organisation he found these events a little stressful, partly because he was a perfectionist and assumed that others would always notice the less-than-perfect aspects of his work but also because his previous manager always set him extremely challenging targets. When the event finally came around, he was astonished at the difference in approach. His new manager asked what his overall goals were and discussed targets with him. Then asked if there was anything he had already achieved that he could include in the paperwork as that would take the pressure off and allow him to be 'ahead of the game'. They finally agreed on three quite basic targets that Alejandro knew he could achieve with very little effort, and he left the meeting with mixed feelings about the process. On the one hand, it was far less painful than meetings with his previous manager, but on the other he felt a little flat as he didn't really have anything to strive for.

According to Locke and Latham (1990) the setting of clear goals and targets has a significant impact on both performance and motivation but only if they are specific and challenging. Most people are familiar with the SMART model for setting targets, which requires that targets are specific, measurable, achievable, relevant and time-bound. This provides a general framework and is a very popular approach perhaps because of its apparent simplicity, but in my experience there are two key issues with the SMART approach. The first is that writing specific and measurable targets is much more difficult than people imagine and often targets are written in the form of tasks to complete. The second is that the system is often used to set targets which are not sufficiently challenging. Alejandro's story isn't particularly unusual. When targets are included in systems such as performance review the focus can be switched to the completion of whatever paperwork is attached to the process rather than really thinking through goals and targets and turns what could be a very meaningful discussion into a tick box activity.

Locke and Latham (1990) suggest that if we do not approach goal setting in the right way, it may impact negatively on motivation and we will simply be outlining tasks to complete rather than specific goals to strive for. A suggested framework to support the process would include:

- *Clarity* – For a goal to be motivating it needs to be clear and the outcome should be measurable.
- *Challenge* – Goals need to have the right amount of challenge. One that is too easy to achieve is unlikely to motivate and won't improve performance. Equally one that is seen as being too difficult could be overwhelming.
- *Commitment* is an essential requirement if goals are to be worthwhile, therefore personal goals should be 'ecological' in that they should be a good fit for the individual, and goals set within a professional framework need to be negotiated so that they are appropriate for the individual and the organisation.
- *Feedback* helps the process of goal setting in that it provides acknowledgement of progress or highlights adjustments that are required. When setting goals individually, feedback will become a part of the reflective process.
- *Task complexity* – whilst goals need to be challenging, they also need to be achievable, so the right level of task complexity is key. Deciding on level of challenge can be difficult as what constitutes pressure for one person can be very different to another. The inverted U model, although now more than 100 years old, still illustrates this clearly (Yerkes & Dodson, 1908; Figure 10.3).

When goals are quite specific, using a target setting approach is a good way to break the overall goal down into steps and allows us to measure progress easily. However, some goals might be about embedding things into our practice, rather than simply achieving a set outcome. For example, we may want to create a long-term change, such as the way we work with colleagues. This isn't a one-off goal that once achieved we then shelve. It is something that will continue as a natural part of our practice. For this type of goal, we may need to change our whole approach, so rather than setting specific targets, consider the framework in which activities take place and make small changes to the habits that form our daily routines.

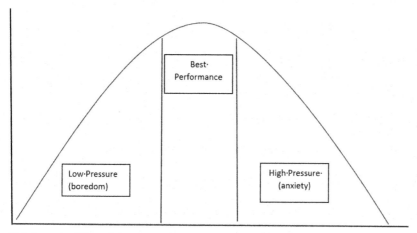

Figure 10.3 Inverted U model

Habitual behaviours

As we have discussed in previous chapters, much of our behaviour is habitual and when it comes to our work there is a tendency to stick with tried and tested methods. Habits in the workplace form part of our learned experience. Sometimes they come about as a result of thinking through what we do, sometimes they are formed in response to organisational pro-cesses and sometimes they just evolve over time. Habits are part of our procedural memory, the part of the memory that allows us to execute tasks without conscious thought such as, throwing a ball, typing or steering a car. They also form a part of our standard routine, such as making a cup of tea when you get up or when you start work or always checking emails before you do anything else. Once they are embedded, we don't think too much about these actions and do the same thing in the same way each time.

   This is fine when our habits are working for us, but there are times when we need to adapt to a changing environment. Sometimes this requires a slight adaptation to what we do; sometimes it requires a complete rethink. I recall the days, long ago, when electronic typewriters were being replaced by PCs. At that time the word processing package would offer tips of the day which helped to develop the user's knowledge of the package. My boss's PA was so enamoured with this facility that she asked the IT support team if they could access the program and print out all of the 'tips of the day' for her so that she could have a hard copy. They declined. Her habit was to read from paper not from a screen, so she copied down each tip by hand and began to compile a list – it hadn't occurred to her to store the tips electronically and access them as and when she needed to. This would simply have required a slight tweak in her practice, however, acknowledging the differences between paper-based and electronic systems was a much bigger thing and needed a complete rethink. Changing how we think about things is a challenge. Similarly changing habits of practice requires a sustained effort.

Making habit your friend

Habitual behaviours don't need to be negative. We also develop some useful habits which may help in overall achievement of goals. Prolific writer Haruki Marukami is well -known for writing ten pages a day, then going for a run before undertaking the rest of the day's activities (Marukami, 2014). Similarly, another prolific writer, Anthony Trollope, used to write in short bursts consistently writing for 15 minutes, several times a day, every day. These are positive habits that formed part of a daily routine, so were undertaken as a matter of course and probably with very little thought. By setting up positive habits which provide small incremental steps towards overall goals we are working on them without much apparent effort. It simply becomes a part of what we do. As Durrant says: 'We are what we repeatedly do. Excellence, then is not an act but a habit' (Durrant, 1926: 74).

Taking this approach switches the focus from achievement of an overall and probably distant goal, to setting up a system that supports that goal (Clear, 2018). By creating small habits which form incremental steps towards overall aims it is possible to build a framework which will support achievement. The framework should be built out of easy steps and form part of an overall routine, so it would be triggered by another event in the daily schedule. For example, if your goal was to get toned thighs, one way to do this might be to set up a punishing exercise routine and a restrictive diet. In all probability, this would be done for a while until something created a hurdle, perhaps an indulgent weekend or an injury. If instead you decided to create a system for the change this would involve embedding some smaller habits, attached to other routines in your day-to-day activities, such as doing some squats before breakfast, and going for a walk in the afternoon before you check your emails. Building small activities into your habitual daily pattern makes them much easier to accommodate, so they are likely to be sustained. Butler *et al.* (2018) suggest there are five steps to creating new habits:

1   Decide what your new habit will be – be clear about the behaviour you will repeat so that it becomes automatic. For example, spend 15 minutes practising yoga every morning before breakfast.
2   Create simple and realistic rules to follow – what can you do without it feeling like an effort. For example, I will listen to my language course CD whenever I drive to work.
3   Identify the cue – to make a habit stick it needs to be linked to a cue so that repetition becomes automatic. In example 1, the cue is breakfast (yoga happens before breakfast), and the cue in example 2 is driving to work, which becomes associated with listening to the language CD.
4   Establish a pre-habit ritual – this helps with the transition between activities. Often selecting something enjoyable is a good choice as that makes it much easier to establish, so you might relax with a cup of tea before practising yoga.
5   Create the right environment – make it pleasant and easy to adopt your new habit. Have what you need to hand and limit distractions.

The key to establishing habits is to set them up so that you can't fail. This means preparing what you need, attaching the habit to other, already embedded rituals and making sure that expectations are realistic.

The limitations of positive thinking

Positive thinking certainly has its place, and there are numerous references to is merit (Dweck, 2017; Byrne, 2006; Seligman, 2018). Indeed, many studies have shown that there are a number of benefits to thinking positively, particularly in relation to how we view future events. People who are able to think optimistically about the future generally enjoy better health, more fulfilling relationships and greater success (Sweeney, 2017). However, as outlined in Chapter 4, positivity isn't a magic spell and although advocates of the law of attraction might have us think otherwise, simply requesting that the power of the universe meet our needs might not be the best approach. Whilst it is important to avoid forms of distorted thinking (outlined in Chapter 4) and to consider our explanatory style, as discussed in Chapter 5, we probably need to do a little more than just think positively.

Using the power of positive thinking might well inspire us and motivate action towards goals, but it will not prepare us for the hurdles that are likely to be presented, and research suggests that it is not only important to imagine a positive outcome but also to think practically about the potential barriers to achieving that outcome (Oettingham, 2014). *Mental contrasting* is a self-regulation strategy that can help us to do this in goal setting. This involves imagining a desired future outcome and then contrasting that with the reality of achieving that outcome, so we might visualise our goal but then do the same in relation to obstacles that may present themselves. This helps us to prepare for potential obstacles and improves overall self-efficacy. A suggested approach to practical goal achievement is WOOP:

Wish - tune in to what you want to achieve and get a clear sense of what that would look and feel like.
Outcome - create a clear and specific goal, usually something measurable so that you know you have achieved it.
Obstacles - imagine the route from where you are now to where you want to be and consider what obstacles might be encountered (thoughts, emotions, habits, other people).
Plan - imagine what difficulties might present themselves and then plan how you will overcome them. Using the *If and then* approach is helpful here . . . if (a particular difficulty) arises, then I will. . . . This helps to mentally rehearse potential hurdles and prepare ways of overcoming them, so it has both a practical and psychological benefit.

Chapter reflections

In this chapter we have considered the importance of turning reflection into action. Whilst it is acknowledged that reflection in itself has inherent value, in professional practice it is important that it is used in ways which not only improve our own practice but which, when shared with others, can have a positive impact on the profession overall. Throughout the book we have acknowledged the importance critically analysing our thinking as well as our actions and in doing so not only to challenge our own beliefs and assumptions but also challenge the basis of hegemonic practice.

References

Butler, G., Grey, N., & Hope, T. (2018) *Managing Your Mind, The Mental Fitness Guide* (3rd ed.). Oxford: Oxford University Press.

Byrne, R. (2006). *The Secret*. New York, NY: Atria Books.

Clear, J. (2018) *Atomic Habits: An Easy and Proven Way to Build Good Habits and Break Bad Ones*. London: Random House Business.

Durrant, W. (1926) *The Story of Philosophy*. Available at: https://archive.org/details/THESTORYOF-PHILOSOPHY1TheLivesAndOpinionswillDurant1926/page/n105/mode/2up?q=We+are+what+we+repeatedly+do. [date accessed 12/1/21] www.poetryverse.com/ts-eliot-poems/four-quartets-burnt-norton.

Dweck, C. (2017) *Mindset – Changing the Way You Think to Fulfil Your Potential*. UK, London: Constable and Robinson Ltd.

Eliot, T. S. (1936) *Four Quartets*. New York: Harcourt.

Locke, E. A., & Latham, G. P. (1990) *A Theory of Goal Setting and Task Performance*. Englewood Cliffs, NJ: Prentice Hall.

Marukami, H. (2014) *Men without Women*. London: Vintage.

Oettingham, G. (2014) *Rethinking Positive Thinking: Inside The New Science of Motivation*. New York, NY: Penguin Publishing Group.

Seligman, M (2018) *Learned Optimism: How to Change Your Mind and Your Life*. London: Nicholas Brealey Publishing.

Sweeney, K. (2017) 'The Downsides of Positivity'. Available at: The downsides of positivity | The Psychologist (bps.org.uk) [date accessed 16/1/21].

Yerkes, R. M., & Dodson, J. D. (1908) 'The Relation of Strength and Stimulus to Rapidity of Habit Formation'. *Journal of Comparative Neurology and Psychology*, 459(18): 482.

Final thoughts

The premise of this book was to provide practical strategies which could easily be incorporated into reflective practice. As suggested in the introduction, a further aim was to offer a 'mirror' to readers so that they may see something of themselves within the pages and be able to use these insights to implement desired changes. Whilst change is important, it isn't always about finding an immediate solution to a problem or a quick-fix innovation. Instead, it requires resourcefulness, the ability to think flexibly and the persistence to work with issues until we are able to use our expertise to make the right changes. By recognising the value in different perspectives and alternative approaches, we become more resourceful. This, coupled with the humility to acknowledge that we don't have all the answers, provides us with the capacity to change what we do as well as how we think about things.

An important element of reflection is the recognition of the everyday, the 'ordinary' events that form the fabric of our lives. These often overlooked gems may offer even more opportunities for insight, which reminds me of a story . . .

A group of travellers had been asked to collect pebbles, something they saw as pointless until the pebbles turned into diamonds. When reflecting on their experience, the travellers considered the difference between something they had considered worthless and then extremely valuable. This reflection, when applied in a wider sense, made them wonder how many other things in their lives which they had previously considered to be of little or no consequence might actually have a value that they hadn't yet discovered. As a result, 'they began to get more and more curious about discovering meanings under the surface of things, which only now were they beginning to comprehend' (Hodgson, 2010: x).

Your reflections may not always uncover diamonds, but there are opportunities for learning woven into the events of everyday life. These are things we may choose to notice, or we may let them pass us by.

Reference

Hodgson, D. (2010) *Magic of Modern Metaphor, Walking with the Stars*. Wales: Crown House Publishing.

DOI: 10.4324/9781003056812-12

Appendix

Overview of 5- and 10-minute reflection strategies

Chapter (strategy no)	Strategy Description and Purpose
1 (strategy 1)	**5-Minute Strategy - Downloading** Spend five minutes writing down your thoughts about the day. Do not edit them, just write until the time is up. When you have finished, go back and highlight anything that seems significant in terms of the words you have chosen. Are there any words repeated? Have you focussed on particular aspects of the day? Are there any connections between the two? Do any metaphors fit today's story? **Purpose** The downloading activity is a strategy for gathering unedited thoughts in order to analyse the language you are using. This provides a clue to the sorts of stories being created about particular events and may offer some nuggets for further reflection. What is particularly useful about this strategy is the process of editing written work - in doing this we really have to think about our choice of words and have the opportunity to analyse our perception of events. It is a starting point to criticality.
1 (strategy 2)	**10-Minute strategy - What/So what/Now What?** Think back over the last week and pick out an event that has troubled you. It doesn't have to be a big event, just something that prompted you to think a little more than usual. Using the structure and questions outlined in the What? So what? Now what? approach outlined in chapter one, explore the event in a little more detail. **Purpose** This strategy encourages objective thought about an event and is a practical approach leading to potential actions. By outlining the event and exploring what it means we can then consider potential actions.
2 (strategy 3)	**10-Minute Strategy - Video Replay** This activity requires you to be in a relaxed state, so it may be best to start with a few deep breaths or a yoga move or two - whatever does the trick for you! Once relaxed, re-run the events of the week through your mind as if you are watching a video replay of them. As you do this, notice any tensions or positive feelings. Just go with it, no judgement or analysis. Simply let the video play out. When you have finished, jot down notes of the most vivid images and note any emotions that were apparent during the replay. **Purpose** This strategy provides an opportunity to review experiences objectively and to focus on details, in particular noticing how we feel about any particular incidents.

Chapter (strategy no)	Strategy Description and Purpose

3 (strategy 4)   **10-Minute Strategy - Johari's Window**

This can be a powerful tool for examining aspects of ourselves we keep hidden or are not in our awareness. Ideally, the tool should be used with support from someone you trust to help you explore (such as a friend or mentor), but it can quite easily be done alone and then discussed at a later date. Using the example quadrant in Figure 3.4 as a guide, draw up your own quadrant as honestly as you can. Then when you are ready, discuss this with someone else. Remember this is not about judgement, it is simply about bringing things into awareness so that they may be explored further.

Purpose

This strategy improves self-knowledge through self-disclosure and feedback and brings into awareness things which may have previously been hidden.

4 (strategy 5)   **10-Minute Strategy - Down the rabbit hole**

1 Write down your assumptions (no editing)
2 Ask why - what is the reason for the assumption?
3 Examine the words . . . what are the meanings behind the words? Could these be redefined?
4 Hypothesise - imagine an assumption is removed. What would happen? What if you changed an aspect of it or replaced it with a different assumption?
5 Follow your thoughts down the rabbit hole by repeating each step to uncover further assumptions.

Purpose

A strategy which provides a framework for analysing assumptions. Steps can be repeated with different assumptions.

4 (strategy 6)   **5-Minute Strategy - Doodling**

Take your focus away from your conscious thoughts by spending five minutes doodling or colouring something in. Choose something that doesn't require you to think too much, simply get engrossed in the activity.

Purpose

This is a way of creating an incubation period by doing something at a level of unconscious competence and occupying your conscious brain with the task in hand to allow space for unconscious processing.

5 (strategy 7)   **5-Minute Strategy - What not Why?**

When we examine thoughts and feelings or consider the way we behaved in a particular situation we often do this from the perspective of why? Why did I say that thing? Why did I do that? Why am I feeling this way? In doing this we will be seeking believable answers - and often what makes them believable is that that confirm what we already 'know'. In your next reflection try switch the why questions for what questions. For example, 'What did I say?', 'What was I feeling?', even 'What was good about that?', 'What could have been better?'

Purpose

'Why?' is an ineffective question in terms of raising self-awareness as we don't have access to all of the unconscious thoughts and feelings that inform our actions and tend to create answers that might feel true for us (but can be wrong). Asking 'what?' allows us to stay objective as we are no forcing judgements in order to answer the questions.

Chapter (strategy no)	Strategy Description and Purpose

5 (strategy 8)   **10-Minute Strategy – Feared Fantasy**

Step one – write down all the negative thoughts you think others might be having about you. The sort of things that people might ordinarily think but wouldn't say. Be honest – what are your most feared judgements?

Step two – write out a dialogue between a critic and yourself. The aim is for the critic to highlight your feared judgements in a very direct way and for you to respond with a combination of self-defence and acceptance. In self-defence you will let your critic know that what they are saying isn't true. Then using acceptance, you will agree with the critic with a sense of humour and inner peace. For example:

Critic: 'You can be really difficult to work with. Why do you always have to disagree with things?'

You: 'That may be true, but the way I see it, I am bringing a different perspective.'

Critic: 'That's what you call it! Honestly, it's a wonder you still have a job. Why can't you just shut up and get on with it?'

You: 'I imagine a lot of my colleagues want to say that to me . . . but I care about what I do and I think it is important that we consider a range of options. Overall, this has to improve our decision-making.'

Purpose

This technique is really a way of dealing with the projection of your own self-critical thoughts. In a sense it is doing battle with yourself. A key aim is that you can move into the acceptance mode and not spend the whole conversation in self-defence – so that by accepting the self-criticism and not feeling the need to defend it you make it less powerful.

6 (strategy 9)   **10-Minute Strategy – A Letter to a Stranger**

Select the most difficult event of the week. Then write a letter to a stranger outlining what happened, what you thought and felt about the event and what impact it has had on you. Remember the stranger has no significance in your life other than being the recipient of your letter.

Purpose

By writing a letter about a difficult event, we put ourselves in the position of thinking carefully about sequence and need to express thoughts with clarity, which in turn can aid objectivity. There is also a purpose in this being a letter to a stranger: if we don't have a relationship, we have no role in that person's life and are not concerned with impression management, therefore, our description is likely to be honest and will not be influenced by any expectations of the relationship.

6 (strategy 10)   **5-Minute Strategy – Judgement Reframe**

Think of a recent event where you have made a firm judgement about someone or something. You may have judged someone on how they dealt with something, on their appearance, or on the way they spoke to you. First write down your initial judgement without editing it. Then reframe it by asking yourself 'What else could this mean?', 'What purpose did this behaviour serve?'

Purpose

This is an easy strategy for helping to reframe the way we think about things. By asking the questions 'What else could this mean?' we are forced to think about alternatives and by asking 'What purpose did this behaviour serve?' we must consider the positive intention behind the behaviour which helps our overall understanding in context.

Chapter (strategy no)	Strategy Description and Purpose
7 (strategy 11)	**5-Minute Strategy - Making Connections** Select two unrelated objects within your house - for example a cooking utensil and a product you use in your skincare routine. Without editing your ideas, write down any ways you can think of combining these two objects. **Purpose** The purpose of this reflective strategy is to encourage divergent thinking. By removing familiar combinations, we are creating space for new ways of seeing things and have the potential to think about them in a completely different way.
7 (strategy 12)	**10-Minute Strategy - Sliding Doors** This strategy is based on the 1998 film of the same name in with a woman's love life and career are closely connected to whether or not she catches a specific train. As the film progresses, we see each story play out. Consider an event or opportunity, for example, a prospective new job that you are considering, a personal goal, or maybe something associated to a pertinent relationship. Using your imagination create a script with various options. What possible opportunities will present themselves? What potential hurdles might you come across? How does the story end in the different scripts? **Purpose** The purpose of this strategy is to think through a range of possibilities. When considering a course of action this might help to test out potential options to see if they are a good fit for us. By creating a story, we are also extending our thinking beyond the issue itself and can test out the routes that feel right. Really letting our imagination run free is the key to success with this strategy - if we constrain it then we are likely to opt for the well-trodden path of familiarity and by default take similar actions which most likely result in similar outcomes.
7 (strategy 13)	**5-Minute strategy - Artfully Vague Fantasy** Read this passage at a relaxed pace and focus your attention inwards noticing your reactions to it. As you sit back and relax, I wonder if you can imagine some restful, peaceful place? Begin to relax your body for this journey. Where is your journey taking you? What do you see? What can you hear? Paying attention to your breathing. What small things do you notice? Whilst you might be wondering which path to take, you might begin to get curious about your journey. As you begin to imagine a place where your mind is free to flow, your mind is now becoming more open to the idea of change, making the connections you have to make. As you meander along your chosen path you begin to notice . . . **Purpose** Artfully vague language is intended to provide a trance-like state that is individual, similar to that you might experience when involved in an activity you can complete with unconscious competence - something you do regularly that requires no direct thinking, for example, walking, riding a bike or driving. The choice of language is deliberately vague so that no thoughts or ideas are imposed and the journey can be taken in any direction.

Chapter (strategy no)	Strategy Description and Purpose

8 (strategy 14)

10-Minute Reflection – Once Upon a Time

Take a look at the seven basic plots outlined in Chapter 8 and select the one you are most drawn to. Then, using the basic tenets of the plot, construct a personal story. What patterns do you recognise? What does this tell you about how you are constructing your own story?

Purpose

The purpose of this activity is to help locate patterns within our own stories. By plotting life's events in this way, we may also locate aspects of connection, pertinent twists in the tale and crossroads which led to certain decisions.

8 (strategy 15)

10-Minute Reflection – 5 Steps

1 Outline a problem, concern or event that you have been thinking about.
2 List as many aspects of it as you can. Write down anything you have any information about and list each thing separately.
3 Go back over the list and highlight any connections between the various parts.
4 Then look for common themes or repeating patterns.
5 Finally, rewrite the event or concern.

Purpose

The purpose of this activity is to search out connections and patterns which may ultimately help us to redefine a concern. This is based on the premise that our initial reflection (in point 1) may well be based on a story we are telling ourselves and the rewrite in point 5 has the benefit of having outlined connections and patterns. The outlines in points 1 and 5 may well end up being the same, which simply means that the initial concern was objectively recorded.

9 (stratergy 16)

10-Minute Reflection – Value Checker

Think about a positive event that was meaningful for you. How did you feel? What values were being met by this event? Write down as many as come to mind. Now, flip this around to a time when you felt angry, frustrated or upset. How did you feel? What values were being surpressed by this event?

Purpose

The purpose of this activity is to highlight the core values that link to our feelings. It is possible that you may have a big list, in which case try grouping them until you can whittle the list down a little.

10 (strategy 17)

10-Minute Strategy – Mindmap

Using your preferred method of mindmapping, reflect on the things you would like to change. Try to think of several areas where you might like to make changes and make each one of these a branch on your map. Then consider the framework required for these changes and add those to the relevant branches. Mindmaps can be a creative process, so the use of colour and images is helpful.

Purpose

Mindmaps present a graphical organiser and allow you to get your thoughts down as they occur to you, then add to them as you follow a train of thought through. They are a great way of exploring new topics, generating ideas or simply organising your thoughts and have the benefit of being able to accommodate a lot of information on a single sheet.

10 (strategy 18)

5-Minute Reflection – Stream of Consciousness Writing

Briefly think about the things that may work for you in the reflective process. Then set a timer for five minutes and write uninterrupted. Write whatever comes to mind and ignore normal conventions such as punctuation and spelling. It doesn't matter if the words or thoughts lack coherence, as they are likely to do this quite naturally.

Chapter (strategy no)	Strategy Description and Purpose
	Purpose
	Stream of consciousness writing is often used in literature to portray an individual's point of view. The key idea is that the writing occurs in a flow and is not disturbed by any form of editing. It can also be used as a therapeutic tool as it is completely uncensored. We all have disconnected thoughts and feelings that often go unacknowledged because we can't make sense of them. This strategy allows them to be recorded, and they may be reviewed at a later date when things do begin to make more sense.
10 (strategy 19)	**5-Minute Reflection – No Limits**
	Write down your ideas in relation to the following statement:
	'If there were absolutely no limits, what would I choose to do?'
	It is important to allow free thought without imposing any limits. The focus is on what you want to do, not what you can or should do.
	Purpose
	Habitual ways of thinking and doing provide a sense of security but they also impose limits. When we try to generate ideas within the framework of what we normally think and do, then we are automatically limiting our options for development. The 'no limits' reflection provides the scope to look beyond what is current and has a focus on extending our thinking to allow the generation of new ideas. There are some similar strategies in Chapter 7, in which we considered the ways that reflection can be used to enhance creativity.

INDEX

Note: **Bold** page numbers indicate a table on the corresponding page. *Italic* page numbers indicate a figure on the corresponding page. Page numbers with a 'n' plus a number indicate a note on the corresponding page.